THE DIARY OF A
U-BOAT COMMANDER

"We rammed a destroyer, passing through her like a knife through cheese."

" . . . they are so black and swift I don't go near them."

Anonymous

The Diary of a U-boat Commander

With an Introduction and Explanatory
Notes by Etienne
and
18 Illustrations on Art Paper by
Frank H. Mason.

BOOKS BY ETIENNE

STRANGE TALES FROM THE FLEET
A NAVAL LIEUTENANT
1914—1918.

"In collaboration with Navallus.
Five Songs from the Grand Fleet."

BIBLIOBAZAAR

Copyright © BiblioBazaar, LLC

BiblioBazaar Reproduction Series: Our goal at BiblioBazaar is to help readers, educators and researchers by bringing back in print hard-to-find original publications at a reasonable price and, at the same time, preserve the legacy of literary history. The following book represents an authentic reproduction of the text as printed by the original publisher and may contain prior copyright references. While we have attempted to accurately maintain the integrity of the original work(s), from time to time there are problems with the original book scan that may result in minor errors in the reproduction, including imperfections such as missing and blurred pages, poor pictures, markings and other reproduction issues beyond our control. Because this work is culturally important, we have made it available as a part of our commitment to protecting, preserving and promoting the world's literature.

All of our books are in the "public domain" and many are derived from Open Source projects dedicated to digitizing historic literature. We believe that when we undertake the difficult task of re-creating them as attractive, readable and affordable books, we further the mutual goal of sharing these works with a larger audience. A portion of Bibliobazaar profits go back to Open Source projects in the form of a donation to the groups that do this important work around the world. If you would like to make a donation to these worthy Open Source projects, or would just like to get more information about these important initiatives, please visit www.bibliobazaar.com/opensource.

The Diary of a
U-boat Commander

LIST OF ILLUSTRATIONS

"We rammed a destroyer, passing through her like a knife through cheese" 2
" . . . they are so black and swift I don't go near them" 2
"Steering north-westerly . . . to lay a small minefield off Newcastle" . 33
"He had suddenly seen the bow waves of a destroyer approaching at full speed to ram" 33
"We were put down by a trawler at dawn" 51
"The torpedo had jumped clean out of the water a hundred yards short of the steamer and had then dived under her" 50
"A moment later there was a severe jar; we had struck the bottom" ... 51
"As the dim lights on the mole disappeared, the ceaseless fountain of star-shells, mingling with the flashing of guns, rose inland on our port beam" 68
"We hit her aft for the second time . . ." 68
"The track met our ram" 84
"In the flash I caught a glimpse of his conning tower" 84
"The 1,000 kilogrammes of metal crashed down" 109
"Good-bye! Steer west for America!" 110
"It is a snug anchorage, and here I intend to remain" 110
"A trapdoor near her bows fell down, the White Ensign was broken at the fore, and a 4-inch gun opened fire from the embrasure that was revealed on her side" 135
"I sighted two convoys, but there were destroyers there . . ." 136
" . . . when there was a blinding flash and the air seemed filled with moaning fragments" 152

"When I put up my periscope at 9 a.m. the horizon seemed to be ringed with patrols" 152

* * * * *

INTRODUCTION

"I would ask you a favour," said the German captain, as we sat in the cabin of a U-boat which had just been added to the long line of bedraggled captives which stretched themselves for a mile or more in Harwich Harbour, in November, 1918.

I made no reply; I had just granted him a favour by allowing him to leave the upper deck of the submarine, in order that he might await the motor launch in some sort of privacy; why should he ask for more?

Undeterred by my silence, he continued: "I have a great friend, Lieutenant-zu-See Von Schenk, who brought U.122 over last week; he has lost a diary, quite private, he left it in error; can he have it?"

I deliberated, felt a certain pity, then remembered the *Belgian Prince* and other things, and so, looking the German in the face, I said:

"I can do nothing."

"Please."

I shook my head, then, to my astonishment, the German placed his head in his hands and wept, his massive frame (for he was a very big man) shook in irregular spasms; it was a most extraordinary spectacle.

It seemed to me absurd that a man who had suffered, without visible emotion, the monstrous humiliation of handing over his command intact, should break down over a trivial incident concerning a diary, and not even his own diary, and yet there was this man crying openly before me.

It rather impressed me, and I felt a curious shyness at being present, as if I had stumbled accidentally into some private recess of his mind. I closed the cabin door, for I heard the voices of my crew approaching.

He wept for some time, perhaps ten minutes, and I wished very much to know of what he was thinking, but I couldn't imagine how it would be possible to find out.

I think that my behaviour in connection with his friend's diary added the last necessary drop of water to the floods of emotion which he had striven, and striven successfully, to hold in check during the agony of handing over the boat, and now the dam had crumbled and broken away.

It struck me that, down in the brilliantly-lit, stuffy little cabin, the result of the war was epitomized. On the table were some instruments I had forbidden him to remove, but which my first lieutenant had discovered in the engineer officer's bag.

On the settee lay a cheap, imitation leather suit-case, containing his spare clothes and a few books. At the table sat Germany in defeat, weeping, but not the tears of repentance, rather the tears of bitter regret for humiliations undergone and ambitions unrealized.

We did not speak again, for I heard the launch come alongside, and, as she bumped against the U-boat, the noise echoed through the hull into the cabin, and aroused him from his sorrows. He wiped his eyes, and, with an attempt at his former hardiness, he followed me on deck and boarded the motor launch.

Next day I visited U.122, and these papers are presented to the public, with such additional remarks as seemed desirable; for some curious reason the author seems to have omitted nearly all dates. This may have been due to the fear that the book, if captured, would be of great value to the British Intelligence Department if the entries were dated. The papers are in the form of two volumes in black leather binding, with a long letter inside the cover of the second volume.

Internal evidence has permitted me to add the dates as regards the years. My thanks are due to K. for assistance in translation.

ETIENNE.

* * * *

THE DIARY OF A U-BOAT COMMANDER

One volume of my war-journal completed, and I must confess it is dull reading.

I could not help smiling as I read my enthusiastic remarks at the outbreak of war, when we visualized battles by the week. What a contrast between our expectations and the actual facts.

Months of monotony, and I haven't even seen an Englishman yet.

Our battle cruisers have had a little amusement with the coast raids at Scarborough and elsewhere, but we battle-fleet fellows have seen nothing, and done nothing.

So I have decided to volunteer for the U-boat service, and my name went in last week, though I am told it may be months before I am taken, as there are about 250 lieutenants already on the waiting list.

But sooner or later I suppose something will come of it.

I shall have no cause to complain of inactivity in that Service, if I get there.

* * * * *

I am off to-night for a six-days trip, two days of which are to be spent in the train, to the Verdun sector.

It has been a great piece of luck. The trip had been arranged by the Military and Naval Inter-communication Department; and two officers from this squadron were to go.

There were 130 candidates, so we drew lots; as usual I was lucky and drew one of the two chances.

It should be intensely interesting.

*****

At—

I arrived here last night after a slow and tiresome journey, which was somewhat alleviated by an excellent bottle of French wine which I purchased whilst in the Champagne district.

Long before we reached the vicinity of Verdun it was obvious to the most casual observer that we were heading for a centre of unusual activity.

Hospital trains travelling north-east and east were numerous, and twice our train, which was one of the ordinary military trains, was shunted on to a siding to allow troop trains to rumble past.

As we approached Verdun the noise of artillery, which I had heard distantly once or twice during the day, as the casual railway train approached the front, became more intense and grew from a low murmur into a steady noise of a kind of growling description, punctuated at irregular intervals by very deep booms as some especially heavy piece was discharged, or an ammunition dump went up.

The country here is very different from the mud flats of Flanders, as it is hilly and well wooded. The Meuse, in the course of centuries, has cut its way through the rampart of hills which surround Verdun, and we are attacking the place from three directions. On the north we are slowly forcing the French back on either river bank—a very costly proceeding, as each wing must advance an equal amount, or the one that advances is enfiladed from across the river.

We are also slowly creeping forward from the east and north-east in the direction of Douaumont.

I am attached to a 105-cm. battery, a young Major von Markel in command, a most charming fellow. I spent all to-day in the advanced observing position with a young subaltern called Grabel, also a nice young fellow. I was in position at 6 a.m., and, as apparently is common here, mist hides everything from view until the sun attains a certain strength. Our battery was supporting the attack on the north side of the river, though the battery itself was on the south side, and firing over a hill called L'Homme Mort.

Von Markel told me that the fighting here has not been previously equalled in the war, such is the intensity of the combat and the price each side is paying.

I could see for myself that this was so, and the whole atmosphere of the place is pregnant with the supreme importance of this struggle, which may well be the dying convulsions of decadent France.

His Imperial Majesty himself has arrived on the scene to witness the final triumph of our arms, and all agree that the end is imminent.

Once we get Verdun, it is the general opinion that this portion of the French front will break completely, carrying with it the adjacent sectors, and the French Armies in the Vosges and Argonne will be committed to a general retreat on converging lines.

But, favourable as this would be to us, it is generally considered here that the fall of Verdun will break the moral resistance of the French nation.

The feeling is, that infinitely more is involved than the capture of a French town, or even the destruction of a French Army; it is a question of stamina; it is the climax of the world war, the focal point of the colossal struggle between the Latin and the Teuton, and on the battlefields of Verdun the gods will decide the destinies of nations.

When I got to the forward observing position, which was situated among the ruins of a house, a most amazing noise made conversation difficult.

The orchestra was in full blast and something approaching 12,000 pieces of all sizes were in action on our side alone, this being the greatest artillery concentration yet effected during the war.

We were situated on one side of a valley which ran up at right angles to the river, whose actual course was hidden by mist, which also obscured the bottom of our valley. The front line was down in this little valley, and as I arrived we lifted our barrage on to the far hill-side to cover an attack which we were delivering at dawn.

Nothing could be seen of the conflict down below, but after half an hour we received orders to bring back our barrage again, and Grabel informed me that the attack had evidently failed. This afternoon I heard that it was indeed so, and that one division (the 58th), which had tried to work along the river bank and outflank the hill, had been caught by a concentration of six batteries of French 75's, which were situated across the river. The unfortunate 58th, forced back from the river-side, had heroically fought their way up the side of the hill, only to encounter our barrage, which, owing to the mist, we thought was well above and ahead of where they would be.

Under this fresh blow the 58th had retired to their trenches at the bottom of the small valley. As the day warmed up the mist disappeared, and, like a theatre curtain, the lifting of this veil revealed the whole scene in its terrible and yet mechanical splendour.

I say mechanical, for it all seemed unreal to me. I knew I should not see cavalry charges, guns in the open, and all the old-world panoply of war, but I was not prepared for this barren and shell-torn circle of hills, continually being freshly, and, to an uninformed observer, aimlessly lashed by shell fire.

Not a man in sight, though below us the ground was thickly strewn with corpses. Overhead a few aeroplanes circled round amidst balls of white shell bursts.

During the day the slow-circling aeroplanes (which were artillery observing machines) were galvanized into frightful activity by the sudden appearance of a fighting machine on one side or the other; this happened several times; it reminded me of a pike amongst young trout.

After lunch I saw a Spad shot down in flames, it was like Lucifer falling down from high heavens. The whole scene was enframed by a sluggish line of observation balloons.

Sometimes groups of these would hastily sink to earth, to rise again when the menace of the aeroplane had passed. These balloons seemed more like phlegmatic spectators at some athletic contest than actual participants in the events.

I wish my pen could convey to paper the varied impressions created within my mind in the course of the past day; but it cannot. I have the consolation that, though I think that I have considerable ability as a writer, yet abler pens than mine have abandoned in despair the task of describing a modern battle.

I can but reiterate that the dominant impression that remains is of the mechanical nature of this business of modern war, and yet such an impression is a false one, for as in the past so to-day, and so in the future, it is the human element which is, has been, and will be the foundation of all things.

Once only in the course of the day did I see men in any numbers, and that was when at 3 p.m. the French were detected massing for a counter-attack on the south side of the river. It was doomed to be still-born. As they left their trenches, distant pigmy figures in horizon blue, apparently plodding slowly across the ground, they were lashed by an intensive barrage and the little figures were obliterated in a series of spouting shell bursts.

Five minutes later the barrage ceased, the smoke drifted away and not a man was to be seen. Grabel told me that it had probably cost them 750 casualties. What an amazing and efficient destruction of living organism!

* * * * *

Another most interesting day, though of a different nature.

To-day was spent witnessing the arrangements for dealing with the wounded. I spent the morning at an advanced dressing station on the south bank of the river. It was in a cellar, beneath the ruins of a house, about 400 yards from the front line and under heavy shell-fire, as close at hand was the remains of what had been a wood, which was being used as a concentration point for reserves.

The cover afforded by this so-called wood was extremely slight, and the troops were concentrating for the innumerable attacks and counter-attacks which were taking place under shell fire. This caused the surgeon in charge of the cellar to describe the wood as our main supply station!

I entered the cellar at 8 a.m., taking advantage of a partial lull in the shelling, but a machine-gun bullet viciously flipped into a wooden beam at the entrance as I ducked to go in. I was not sorry to get underground. A sloping path brought me into the cellar, on one side of which sappers were digging away the earth to increase the accommodation.

The illumination consisted of candles set in bottles and some electric hand lamps. The centre of the cellar was occupied by two portable operating tables, rarely untenanted during the three hours I spent in this hell.

The atmosphere—for there was no ventilation—stank of sweat, blood, and chloroform.

By a powerful effort I countered my natural tendency to vomit, and looked around me. The sides of the cellar were lined with figures on stretchers. Some lay still and silent, others writhed and groaned. At intervals, one of the attendants would call the doctor's attention to one of the still forms. A hasty examination ensued, and the stretcher and its contents were removed. A few minutes later the stretcher—empty—returned. The surgeon explained to me that there was no room for corpses in the cellar; business, he genially remarked, was too brisk at the present crucial stage of the great battle.

The first feelings of revulsion having been mastered, I determined to make the most of my opportunities, as I have always felt that the naval officer is at a great disadvantage in war as compared with his military brother, in that he but rarely has a chance of accustoming himself to the unpleasant spectacle of torn flesh and bones.

This morning there was no lack of material, and many of the intestinal wounds were peculiarly revolting, so that at lunch-time, when another convenient lull in the torrent of shell fire enabled me to leave the cellar, I felt thoroughly hardened; in fact I had assisted in a humble degree at one or two operations.

I had lunch at the 11th Army Medical Headquarters Mess, and it was a sumptuous meal to which I did full justice.

After lunch, whilst waiting to be motored to a field hospital, I happened to see a battalion of Silesian troops about to go up to the front line.

It was rather curious feeling that one was looking at men, each in himself a unit of civilization, and yet many of whom were about to die in the interests thereof.

Their faces were an interesting study.

Some looked careless and debonair, and seemed to swing past with a touch of recklessness in their stride, others were grave and serious, and seemed almost to plod forward to the dictates of an inevitable fatalism.

The field hospital, where we met some very charming nurses, on one of whom I think I created a distinct impression, was not particularly interesting. It was clean, well-organized and radiated the efficiency inseparable from the German Army.

* * * * *

Back at Wilhelmshaven—curse it!

Yesterday morning, when about to start on a tour of the ammunition supply arrangements, I received an urgent wire recalling me at once!

There was nothing for it but to obey.

I was lucky enough to get a passage as far as Mons in an albatross scout which was taking dispatches to that place.

From there I managed to bluff a motor car out of the town commandant—a most obliging fellow. This took me to Aachen where I got an express.

The reason for my recall was that Witneisser went sick and Arnheim being away, this has left only two in the operations ciphering department.

My arrival has made us three. It is pretty strenuous work and, being of a clerical nature, suits me little. The only consolation is that many of the messages are most interesting. I was looking through the back files the other day and amongst other interesting information I came across the wireless report from the boat that had sunk the *Lusitania*.

It has always been a mystery to me why we sank her, as I do not believe those things pay.

* * * * *

Arnheim has come back, so I have got out of the ciphering department, to my great delight.

I have received official information that my application for U-boats has been received. Meanwhile all there is to do is to sit at this—hole and wait.

2nd June, 1916.

I have fought in the greatest sea battle of the ages; it has been a wonderful and terrible experience.

All the details of the battle will be history, but I feel that I must place on record my personal experiences.

We have not escaped without marks, and the good old *König* brought 67 dead and 125 wounded into port as the price of the victory off Skajerack, but of the English there are thousands who slept their last sleep in the wrecked hulls of the battle cruisers which will rust for eternal ages upon the Jutland banks.

Sad as our losses are—and the gallant *Lutzow* has sunk in sight of home—I am filled with pride.

We have met that great armada the British Fleet, we have struck them with a hammer blow and we have returned. I was asleep in my cabin when the news came that Hipper was coming south with the British battle cruisers on his beam. In five minutes we were at our action stations. We made contact with Hipper at 5.30 p.m.,[1] and Beatty turned north with his cruisers and fast battleships and we pursued.

Two of the great ships had been sunk by our battle cruisers, and we had hopes of destroying the remainder, when at 6.55 the mist on the northern horizon was pierced by the formidable line of the British Battle Fleet.

Jellicoe had arrived!

Three battle cruisers became involved between the lines, and in an instant one was blown up, and another crawled west in a sinking condition. Sudden and terrible are events in a modern sea-battle.

Confronted with the concentrated force of Britain's Battle Fleet we turned to east, and for twenty minutes our High Seas Fleet sustained the unequal contest.

It was during this period that we were hit seventeen times by heavy shell, though, in my position in the after torpedo control tower, I only realized one hit had taken place, which was when a shell plunged into the after turret and, blowing the roof off, killed every member of the turret's crew.

From my position, when the smoke and dust had blown away, I looked down into a mass of twisted machinery, amongst which I seemed to detect the charred remains of bodies.

At about 7.40 we turned, under cover of our smoke screen, and steered south-west.

---

1 This is 4.30 G.M.T.—Etienne

Our position was not satisfactory, as the last information of the enemy reported them as turning to the southward; consequently they were between us and Heligoland.

At 11 p.m. we received a signal for divisions of battle fleets to steer independently for the Horn Reef swept channel.

Ten minutes later we underwent the first of five destroyer attacks.

The British destroyers, searching wide in the night, had located us, and with desperate gallantry pressed home the attack again and again. So close did they come that about 1.30 a.m. we rammed one, passing through her like a knife through a cheese.

It was a wonderful spectacle to see those sinister craft, rushing madly to their destruction down the bright beam of our powerful searchlights. It was an avenue of death for them, but to the credit of their Service it must stand that throughout the long nightmare they did not hesitate.

The surrounding darkness seemed to vomit forth flotilla after flotilla of these cavalry of the sea.

And they struck us once, a torpedo right forward, which will keep us in dock for a month, but did no vital injury.

When morning dawned, misty and soft, as is its way in June in the Bight, we were to the eastward of the British, and so we came honourably home to Wilhelmshaven, feeling that the young Navy had laid worthy foundations for its tradition to grow upon.

We are to report at Kiel, and shall be six weeks upon the job.

Frankfurt.

Back on seventeen days' leave, and everyone here very anxious to hear details of the battle of Skajerack.

It is very pleasant to have something to talk to the women about. Usually the gallant field greys hold the drawing-room floor, with their startling tales from the Western Front, of how they nearly took Verdun, and would have if the British hadn't insisted on being slaughtered on the Somme.

It is quite impossible in many ways to tell that there is a war on as far as social life in this place is concerned.

There is a shortage of good coffee and that is about all.

* * * * *

Arrived back on board last night.

They have made a fine job of us, and we go through the canal to the Schillig Roads early next week.

We are to do three weeks' gunnery practices from there, to train the new drafts.

1916 *(about August)*.

At last! Thank Heavens, my application has been granted. Schmitt (the Secretary) told me this morning that a letter has come from the Admiralty to say that I am to present myself for medical examination at the board at Wilhelmshaven to-morrow.

What joy! to strike a blow at last, finished for ever the cursed monotony of inactivity of this High Seas Fleet life. But the U-boat war! Ah! that goes well. We shall bring those stubborn, blood-sucking islanders to their knees by striking at them through their bellies.

When I think of London and no food, and Glasgow and no food, then who can say what will happen? Revolt! rebellion in England, and our brave field greys on the west will smash them to atoms in the spring of 1917, and I, Karl Schenk, will have helped directly in this! Great thought—but calm! I am not there yet, there is still this confounded medical board. I almost wish I had not drunk so much last night, not that it makes any difference, but still one must run no risks, for I hear that the medical is terribly strict for the U-boat service. Only the cream is skimmed! Well, to-morrow we shall see.

* * * * *

Passed! and with flying colours; it seemed absurdly easy and only took ten minutes, but then my physique is magnificent, thanks to the physical training I have always done. I am now due to get three weeks' leave, and then to Zeebrugge.

I have wired to the little mother at Frankfurt.

* * * * *

At Zeebrugge, or rather Bruges.

I spent three weeks at home, all the family are pleased except mother; she has a woman's dread of danger; it is a pleasing characteristic in peace time, but a cloy on pleasure in days of war. To her, with the narrowness of a female's intellect, I really believe I am of more importance than the Fatherland—how absurd. Whilst at Frankfurt I saw a good deal of Rosa; she seems better looking each time I meet her; doubtless she is still developing to full womanhood. Moritz was home from Flanders. He had ten days' leave from Ypres, and, though I have a dislike for him, he certainly was interesting, though why the English cling to those wretched ruins is more than I can understand.

I felt instinctively that in a sense Moritz and I were rivals where Rosa was concerned, though I have never considered her in that light—as yet. One day, perhaps? These women are much the same everywhere, and I could see that having entered the U-boat service made a difference with Rosa, though her logic should have told her that I was no different. But is that right? After all, it is something to have joined this service; the Guards themselves have no better cachet, and it is certainly cheaper.

Here we live in billets and in a commandeered hotel. The life ashore is pleasant enough; the damned Belgians are sometimes sulky, but they know who is master. Bissing (a splendid chap) sees to that.

As a matter of fact we have benefited them by our occupation, the shops do a roaring trade at preposterous prices, and shamefully enough the German shopkeepers are most guilty. These pot-bellied merchants don't seem to realize that they exist owing to our exertions.

I was much struck with the beautiful orderliness of the small gardens which we have laid out since 1914, and, in fact, wherever one looks there is evidence of the genius of the German race for thorough organization. Yet these Belgians don't seem to appreciate it. I can't understand it.

I find here that social life is very much gayer than at that mad town of Wilhelmshaven. At the High Seas Fleet bases there was the strictness and austerity that some people seem to consider necessary to show that we are at war, though Heaven knows there was precious little war in the High Seas Fleet; perhaps that was why the "blood and iron" régime was in full order ashore. Here, in Bruges, at any rate as far as the submarine officers are concerned, the matter is far different. When the boats are in, one seems to do as one likes, with a perfunctory visit to the ship in the course of the day.

Witnitz (the Commodore) favours complete relaxation when in from a trip. In the evenings there are parties, for which there are always ladies, and I find it is necessary to have a "smoking."[2] I went to the best tailor to buy one, and found that I must have one made at the damnable price of 140 marks; the fitter, an oily Jew, had the incredible impertinence to assure me it would be cut on London lines!

I nearly felled him to the ground; can one never get away from England and things English? I'll see his account waits a bit before I settle it.

---

2 A dinner jacket.

There are several fellows I know here. Karl Müller, who was 3rd watchkeeper in the *Yorck*, and Adolf Hilfsbaumer, who was captain of G.176, are the two I know best. They are both doing a few trips as second in commands of the later U.C. boats, which are mine-laying off the English coasts. This is a most dangerous operation, and nearly all the U.C. boats are commanded by reserve officers, of whom there are a good many in the Mess.

Excellent fellows, no doubt, but somewhat uncouth and lacking the finer points of breeding; as far as I can see in the short time I have been here they keep themselves to themselves a good deal. I certainly don't wish to mix with them. Unfortunately, it appears that I am almost bound to be appointed as second in command of one of the U.C. boats, for at least one trip before I go to the periscope school and train for a command of my own. The idea of being bottled up in an elongated cigar and under the command of one of those nautical plough-boys is repellent. However, the Von Schenks have never been too proud to obey in order to learn how to command.

* * * * *

I have been appointed second in command to U.C.47. Her captain is one Max Alten by name. Beyond the fact that I saw him drunk one night in the Mess I know nothing of him.

I reported to him and he seems rather in awe of me. His fears are groundless.

I shall make it as easy as possible for him, for it must be as awkward for him as it is unpleasant for me.

To celebrate my proper entry into the U-boat service, I gave a dinner party last night in a private room at "Le Coq d'Or." I asked Karl and Adolf, and told them to bring three girls. My opposite number was a lovely girl called Zoe something or other. I wore my "smoking" for the first time; it is certainly a becoming costume.

We drank a good deal of champagne and had a very pleasant little debauch; the girls got very merry, and I kissed Zoe once. She was not very angry. I think she is thoroughly charming, and I have accepted an invitation to take tea at her flat. She is either the wife or the chère amie of a colonel in the Brandenburgers, I could not make out which. Luckily the gallant "Cockchafer" is at the moment on the La Bassée sector, where I was interested to observe that heavy fighting has broken out to-day. I must console the fair Zoe!

Both Karl and Adolf got rather drunk, Adolf hopelessly so, but I, as usual, was hardly affected. I have a head of iron, provided the liquor is good, and *I* saw to that point.

* * * * *

We were sailing, or rather going down the canal to Zeebrugge on Friday, but the starting resistance of the port main motor burnt out and we were delayed till Sunday, as they will fit a new one.

I must confess the organization for repair work here is admirable, as very little is done by the crews in the U-boats, all work being carried out by the permanent staff, who are quartered at Bruges docks. Taking advantage of the delay I called on Zoe Stein, as I find she is named.

It appears she is *not* married to Colonel Stein. She told me he was fat and ugly, and laughed a good deal about him. She showed me his photograph, and certainly he is no beauty. However, he must be a man of means, as he has given her a charming flat, beautifully decorated with water-colours which the Colonel salved from the French château in the early days—these army fellows had all the chances.

I bade an affectionate farewell to Zoe, and I trust Stein will be still busily engaged at La Bassée when I return in a fortnight's time! I am greatly obliged to Karl for the introduction, and told him so; he himself is running after a little grass widow whose husband has been missing for some months. I think Karl finds it an expensive game; luckily Zoe seems well supplied with money—the essential ingredient in a joyous life.

On Friday night we had an air-raid—a frequent event here, but my first experience in this line. Unpleasant, but a fine spectacle, considerable damage done near the docks and an unexploded bomb fell in a street near our headquarters.

Two machines (British) brought down in flames. I saw the green balls[3] for the first time. A most fascinating sight to see them floating up in waving chains into the vault of heaven; they reminded me of making daisy chains as a child.

At Zeebrugge.

We are alongside the mole in one of the new submarine shelters that has been built.

The boat is under a concrete roof over three feet thick, which would defy the heaviest bomb.

We have much improved the port since our arrival. The port, so-called, is purely artificial, and actually consists of a long mole with a gentle curve in it, which reaches out to seaward and protects the mouth of the canal. The tides are very strong up and down the coast, and constant dredging is carried out to keep 20 feet of water over the sill at the lock gates.

On arrival last night we went straight into No. 11 shelter, as an air-raid was expected, but nothing happened, so I went up to the "Flandre," which seems to be the best hotel here, full of submarine people, and I heard many interesting stories. There seems no doubt this U-boat war is dangerous work; I find the U.C. boats are beginning to be called the Suicide Club, after the famous English story of that name, which, curiously enough, I saw on the kinematograph at Frankfurt last leave.

---

3 Known as "Flying-onions."

We Germans are extraordinarily broad-minded; I doubt if the works of German authors are seen on the screens in England or France.

The news from the West is good, the English are hurling themselves to destruction against our steel front. We are now to load up with mines. I must stop writing to superintend this work.

At sea. Near the South Dogger Light.

We loaded up the ten mines we carry in an hour and five minutes. They were lifted from a railway truck by a big crane and delicately lowered into the mine tubes, of which we have five in the bows.

The tubes extend from the upper deck of the ship to her keel, and slope aft to facilitate release. Having completed with fuel at Bruges, we took in a store of provisions and Alten went up to the Commodore's office to get our sailing orders.

We sailed at 6 p.m. and at last I felt I was off. To-day, the 22nd, we are just north of the South Dogger, steering north-westerly at 9-1/2 knots.

The sea is quite calm and everything is very pleasant. Our mission is to lay a small minefield off Newcastle in the East Coast war channel. I have, of course, never been to sea for any length of time in a U-boat, and it is all very novel.

I find the roar of the Diesel engine very relentless, and last night slept badly in a wretched bunk, which was a poor substitute for my lovely quarters in the barracks at Wilhelmshaven. One thing I appreciate, and that is the food; it is really excellent: fresh milk, fresh butter, white bread and many other luxuries.

I have spent most of the day picking up things about the boat. Her general arrangement is as follows:

Starting in the bows, mine tubes occupy the centre of the boat, leaving two narrow passages, one each side. In the port passage is the wireless cabinet and signal flag lockers, with store rooms underneath. In the starboard passage are one or two small pumps and the kitchen.

The next compartment contains four bunks, two each side, these are occupied by Alten, myself, the engineer, and the Navigating Warrant Officer. Proceeding further aft one enters the control room, in which one periscope is situated, and the necessary valves and pumps for diving the boat.

The next compartment is the crew space; ten of the company exist here.

Overhead on each side is the gear for releasing the torpedoes from the external torpedo tubes, of which we carry one each side. I think we borrowed this idea from the Russians.

Then comes the engine-room, an inferno of rattling noises, but excellent engines, I believe. At the after end of the engine-room are the two main switchboards, of whose manner of working I am at present in some ignorance.

The two main sets of electric motors are underneath the boards, in the stern, where we have a third torpedo tube.

* * * * *

I had hardly written the above words when a message came that the captain would like me to come to the bridge.

I went up in a leisurely fashion, through the conning tower, which is over the control room, and reported myself. He indicated a low-lying patch of smoke on the horizon far away on the starboard bow. I was obliged to confess that it conveyed nothing to me, when he aroused my intense interest by stating that it was, without doubt, being emitted from a British submarine, who are known to frequent these waters. He was proceeding away from us, and was, even then, six or seven miles away, so an attack was out of the question. The engineer, who had joined us, drew my attention to the thin wisp of almost invisible blue-grey smoke from our own stern. The contrast was certainly striking!

Over dinner I gave it as my opinion that the British boats were pretty useless. Alten would not agree, and stated that, though in certain technical aspects they were in a position of inferiority, yet in personnel and skill in attacking they were fully our equals. He seemed to hold them in considerable respect, and he remarked that, when making a passage, he was more anxious on their account than in any other way. He informed me that, on the last passage he made, he was attacked by a British boat which he never saw, the only indication he received being a torpedo which jumped out of the water almost over his tail. Luckily it was very rough at the time, which made the torpedo run erratically, otherwise they would undoubtedly have been hit.

What appeared to astonish him was the fact that the British boat had been able to make an attack in such weather. We are now charging on one engine, 500 amperes on each half-battery.

* * * * *

We are due back at Zeebrugge at 10 p.m. to-night. We should have been in at dawn to-day, but we received a wireless from the senior officer, Zeebrugge, to say that mine-laying was suspected, and we were to wait till the "Q.R." channel, from the Blankenberg buoy, had been swept. We lay in the bottom for eight hours, a few miles from the western end of the channel.

Our trip was quite successful, but not without certain excitements.

On the night of the 23rd we passed fairly close to a fishing fleet on the Dogger Bank, and saw the lights of several steamers in the distance. As our first business was to lay our mines in the appointed place, we did not worry them.

We burnt usual navigation lights, or rather side lights which appear to be usual, except that, by a little fitting which Alten has made himself, the arcs of bearing on which the lights show can be changed at will. His idea is that, should we appear to be approaching a steamer which he wishes to avoid, in many cases, by shining a little more or less red and green light, we can make her think that we are a steamer on such a course that it is her duty by the rules of the road to keep clear of us.

He tells me it has worked on several occasions, and he has also found it useful to have two small auxiliary side lights fitted which are the wrong colours for the sides they are on. It is, of course, only neutral shipping which carry lights nowadays, though Alten says that many British ships are still incredibly careless in the matter of lights.

However, to resume my account of what happened. We reached our position at dawn or slightly after, the weather was beautifully calm and the sea like glass. As we were only three miles from the English coast, and close to the mouth of the Tyne, we were extraordinarily lucky to have nothing in sight, if one excepts a long smudge of smoke which trailed across the horizon to the southward.

The land itself was obscured by early morning banks of mist, yet everything was so still that we actually faintly heard the whistle of a train. I could hardly restrain from suggesting to Alten that we should elevate the 10-cm. gun to fifteen degrees and fire a few rounds on to "proud Albion's virgin shores," but I did not do so as I felt fairly certain that he would not approve, and I do not wish to lay myself open to rebuffs from him after his behaviour concerning the smoking incident. I boil with rage at the thought, but again I digress.

The fact that the land was obscured was favourable from the point of view that we were not worried by coast watchers, but unfavourable from the standpoint that we were unable to take bearings of anything and so ascertain our exact position.

The importance of this point in submarine mine-laying is obvious, for, owing to our small cargo of eggs, it is quite possible that we may be sent here again, to lay an adjacent field, in which case it is highly desirable to know the exact position of one's previous effort.

"Steering north-westerly . . . ; to lay a small minefield off Newcastle."

"He had suddenly seen the bow waves of a destroyer approaching at full speed to ram."

We were somewhat assisted in our efforts to locate ourselves by the fact that a seven-fathom patch existed exactly where we had to lay. We picked up the edge of this bank with our sounding machine, and steering north half a mile, laid our mines in latitude—No! on second thoughts I will omit the precise position, for, though I shall take every precaution, there is no saying that through some misfortune this Journal might not get into the wrong hands.

I am very glad I decided to keep these notes, as I shall take much pleasure in reading them when Victory crowns our efforts and the joys of a peaceful life return.

I found it a delightful sensation being so close to the enemy coast, in his territorial waters, in fact. For the first time since the Skajerack battle I experienced the personal joys of war, the sensation of intimate and successful contact with the enemy, and the most hated enemy at that.

We had hardly finished laying our eggs when a droning noise was heard. With marvellous celerity we dived, that damned fellow Alten, who, under these circumstances leaves the bridge last, treading on my fingers as he followed me down the conning tower ladder.

The engineer endeavoured to sympathize with me, and made some idiotic remark about my being quicker when I had had more practice. I bit his head off. I can't stand this hail-fellow-well-met attitude in these U.C. boats, from any lout dressed in an officer's uniform. They wouldn't be holding commissions if it wasn't for the war, and they should remember that fact. I suppose they think I'm stand-offish. Well, if they had my family tree behind them they would understand.

We dived to sixty feet, and then came up to twenty. Alten looked through the periscope, and then invited me to look. Curiosity impelled me to accept this favour and, putting the focussing lever to "skyscrape" I swept round the sky.

At last I saw him; he was a small gas-bag of diminutive size, beneath which was suspended a little car, the most ridiculous little travesty of an airship I have ever seen. He was nosing along at about 800 feet and making about 40 knots.

Suddenly he must have seen the wake of our periscope, for he turned towards us. Simultaneously Alten, from the conning tower (I was using the other periscope in the control room), ordered the boat to sixty feet, and put the helm hard over.

We had turned sixteen points,[4] and in about two minutes heard a series of reports right astern of us. It was evident that our ruse had succeeded and that he had overshot the mark.

Inside the boat one felt a slight jar as each bomb went off.

We gradually came round to our proper course, and cruised all day submerged at dead slow speed. Every time we lifted our periscope he was still hanging about sufficiently close to make it foolish for us to come to the surface.

Towards noon a group of trawlers, doubtless summoned by wireless, appeared, and proceeded to wander about. These seemed to concern Alten far more than the airship, and he informed me that from their, to me, aimless movements he deduced they were hunting for us by hydroplanes. Occasionally we lay on the bottom in nineteen fathoms.

By 4 p.m. the atmosphere was becoming rather unpleasant and hot, and gradually we took off more clothes. Curiously enough, I longed for a smoke, but wild horses would not have made me ask Alten for permission.

At 8 p.m. it was sufficiently dark to enable us to rise, which gave me great pleasure, though the first rush of fresh air down the hatch made me vomit after hours of breathing the vitiated muck. On coming to the surface we saw nothing in sight, but a breeze had sprung up which caused spray to break over the bridge as we chugged along at 9 knots.

Everyone was in high spirits, as always on the return journey, when the mind turns to the Fatherland and all it holds.

My mind turns to Zoe. I confess it to myself frankly. I hardly realized to what extent this woman had begun to influence me until we received

---

4   180°

the wireless signal ordering us to delay entering for twelve hours. The receipt of this news, trivial though the delay has been, threw a mantle of gloom over the crew. I participated in the depression and, upon thought, rather wondered that this should be so. Self-analysis on the lines laid down by Schessmanweil[5] revealed to me that the basis of my annoyance is the fact that my next meeting with Zoe is deferred! I feel instinctively that I shall have trouble here, and that I had better haul off a lee shore whilst there is manoeuvring room, and yet—and yet I secretly rejoice that every revolution of the propeller, every clank and rattle of the Diesels brings us closer together.

Alten has just come down from the bridge, and we chatted for some moments; it is evident that he wishes to apologize for his rudeness over the smoking incident.

I was in error, I admit it frankly; at the same time I did not know that the battery was on charge, and to dash a match from my hand! I could have shot him where he stood. However, I am not vindictive, and as far as I am concerned the incident is ended.

One thing I find trying in this small boat, and that is that I can find no space in which to do half my Müller exercises, the leg-and-arm-swinging ones. I must see whether I can't invent a set of U-boat exercises!

Good! in two hours we reach the Mole-end light buoy.

* * * * *

Submarine Mess, Bruges.

It is midnight, and as I write in my room at the top of the house the low rumble of the guns from the south-west vibrates faintly through the open window, for it is extraordinarily warm for the time of year, and I have flung back the curtains and risked the light shining.

---

5 Apparently some German author, of obscure origin, as I cannot find him in any book of reference.—ETIENNE.

We spent the night at Zeebrugge and came up to the docks here next day. We shall probably be in for a week, and I am on four days' "extended absence from the boat," which practically means that I can go where I like in the neighbourhood provided I am handy to a telephone.

After a short inward struggle I rang Zoe up on the telephone; fortunately I did not call first.

A man's voice answered, and for a moment I was dumbfounded. I guessed at once it was the Colonel, and I had counted so confidently on his being still away at the front.

For an instant I felt speechless, an impulse came to me to ring off without further ado, but I restrained myself, and then a fine idea came into my head.

"Who is that?" I said.

"Colonel Stein!" replied the voice, and my fears were confirmed, but my plan of campaign held good.

"I am speaking," I continued, "on behalf of Lieutenant Von Schenk—"

"Ah, yes!" growled the voice, and for an instant a panic seized me, but I resumed:

"He met Madame Stein at dinner some days ago, and she kindly asked him to call; he has asked me to ring up and inquire when it would be convenient, as he would like to meet you, sir, as well. He has been unable to ring up himself, as he was sent away from Bruges on duty early this morning."

I smiled to myself at this little lie and listened.

"Your friend had better call to-morrow then, for I leave to-morrow evening for the Somme front; will you tell him?"

I replied that I would, and left the telephone well satisfied, but cursing the fates that made it advisable to keep clear of No. 10, Kafelle Strasse for thirty-six hours. Needless to say next day I rang up again in order to tell the Colonel that Lieutenant Schenk had apparently been detained, as he was not yet back in Bruges, and how I felt sure that he would be sorry at missing the Colonel, etc., etc., but all this camouflage was unnecessary, as she herself came to the 'phone. I could have kissed the instrument when I told her of my stratagem and heard her silvery laughter in my ear.

"It is arranged that to-morrow, starting at 10.30, we motor for the day to the Forest of Meten, taking our lunch and tea with us—pray Heaven the weather holds."

To-night in the Mess it is generally considered that U.B.40 has been lost; she is ten days overdue and was operating off Havre, she has made no signal for a fortnight. Such is the price of victory and the cost of war—death, perhaps, in some terrible form, but bah! away with such thoughts, to-morrow there is love and life and Zoe!

* * * * *

Once more it is night, still the guns rumble on the same old dismal tones, and as it is raining now it must be getting bad up at the front. Except for the rain it might have been last night, but much has happened to me in the meanwhile.

To-day in the forest by Ruysslede I found that I loved Zoe, loved her as I have never yet loved woman, loved her with my soul and all that is me.

The day was gloriously fine when we started, and an hour's run took us to the forest. We left the car at an inn and wandered down one of the glades.

I carried the basket and we strolled on and on until we found a suitable place deep in the heart of the forest.

I have the sailor's love for woods, for their depths, their shadows, their mysteries, which are so vivid a contrast to the monotony of the sea, with the everlasting circle of the horizon and the half-bowl of the heavens above.

In the forest to-day, though the leaves had turned to gold and red and brown, the beeches were still well covered, and overhead we were tented with a russet canopy.

I say, at last we found a spot, or rather Zoe, who, with girlish pleasure in the adventure, had run ahead, called to me, and as I write I seem to hear the echoes of "Karl! Karl!" which rang through the wood. When I came up to her she proudly pointed to the place she had found.

It was ideal. An outcrop of rock formed a miniature Matterhorn in the forest, and beneath its shelter with the old trees as silent witnesses we sat and joked and laughed, and made twenty attempts to light a fire.

After lunch, a little incident happened which had an enormous effect on me; Zoe asked me whether I would mind if she smoked.

How many women in these days would think of doing that? And yet, had she but known it, I am still sufficiently old-fashioned to appreciate the implied respect for any possible prejudices which was contained in her request.

After lunch, I asked her a question to which I dreaded the answer.

I asked her whether, now that the old Colonel had gone to the Somme, whether that meant that she would be leaving Bruges.

She laughed and teasingly said: "Quien sabe, señor," but seeing my real anxiety on this point, she assured me that she was not leaving for the present. The Colonel, she said, had a strange belief that once a man had served on the Flanders Front, and especially on the Ypres salient, he always came back to die there.

It appears that the Colonel has done fourteen months' service on the salient alone, and is firmly convinced he will end his career on that great burial ground. As we were talking about the Colonel I longed to ask her how she had met him, and perhaps find out why she lives with him, for I cannot believe she loves him, but I did not dare.

Strangely enough I found that a curious shyness had taken hold of me with regard to Zoe.

I said to myself, "Fool! you are alone with her, you long to kiss her; you have kissed her, first at the dinner-party, secondly when you said good-bye at her flat," and yet to-day it was different.

Then I was kissing a pretty woman, I was on the eve of a dangerous life, and I was simply extracting the animal pleasures whilst I lived.

To-day it was a case of Zoe, the personality I loved; I still longed to kiss her, but I wanted to have the unquestioned right to kiss her, as much as I wanted the kisses.

I wanted to have her for my own, away from the contaminating ownership of the old Colonel, and I determined to get her.

I think she noticed the changed attitude on my part, and perhaps she felt herself that a subtle change in our relationship had taken place, and whilst I meditated on these things she fell into a doze at my side.

I was sitting slightly above her, smoking to keep the midges away, and as I looked down on her childish figure a great tenderness for her filled my mind. She is very beautiful and to me desirable above all women; I can see her as she lay there trustfully at my feet. I will describe her, and then, when I get her photograph, I will read this when I am far away on a trip.

She is of average height, for I am just over six feet and she reaches to just above my shoulder. Her hair is gloriously thick and of a deep black colour, and lies low on her forehead. Her complexion is of the purest whiteness beyond compare, which but accentuates the red warmth of the lips which encircle her little mouth. Her figure is slight and her ankles are my delight, but her crowning glories, which I have purposely left till last, are her eyes.

I feel I could lose my soul; I have lost it, if I have one, in the violet depths of those eyes, which were veiled as she slept by the long black eyelashes which curled up delicately as they rested on her cheeks. I have re-read this description, and it is oh, so unsatisfying; would I had the pen of a Goethe or a Shakespeare, yet for want of more skill the description shall stand.

How I long for her to be mine, and yet, unfortunate that I am, I cannot for certain declare that she loves me.

A thousand doubts arise. I torment myself with recollections of her behaviour at the dinner-party, when within two hours of our first meeting she gave me her lips.

Yet did I not first roughly kiss her as we danced?

I find consolation in the fact that, though she has said nothing, yet her conduct to-day was different. She was so quiet after tea as we wandered back through the forests with the setting sun striking golden beams aslant the tree trunks.

Before we left I sang to her Tchaikowsky's beautiful song, "To the Forest," and I think she was pleased, for I may say with justice that my voice is of high quality for an amateur, and the song goes well without an accompaniment, whilst the atmosphere and surroundings were ideal.

There was only one jarring note in a perfect day; when we returned to the car the chauffeur permitted himself a sardonic grin. Zoe unfortunately saw it and blushed scarlet.

I could have struck him on his impudent mouth, but for her sake I judged it advisable to notice nothing.

I feel I could go on writing about her all night, but it is nearly 2 a.m. I must get some sleep.

The guns rumble steadily in the south-west, and the sky is lit by their flashes; may the fighting on the Somme be bloody these coming days.

[Probably about ten days later.—Etienne.]

We leave to-night, having had a longer spell than usual. I am in a distracted state of mind. Since our glorious day in the forest I have seen her nearly every afternoon, though twice that swine Alten has kept me in the boat in connection with some replacements of the battery.

I have found out that, like me, she is intensely musical. She plays beautifully on the piano, and we had long hours together playing Chopin and Beethoven; we also played some of Moussorgsky's duets, but I love her best when she plays Chopin, the composer pre-eminent of love and passion.

She has masses of music, as the Colonel gives her what she likes. We also played a lot of Debussy. At first I demurred at playing a living French composer's works, but she pouted and looked so adorable that all my scruples vanished in an instant, so we closed all the doors and she played it for hours very softly whilst I forgot the war and all its horrors and remembered only that I was with the well-beloved girl.

The Colonel writes from Thiepval, where the British are pouring out their blood like water. He writes very interesting letters, and has had many narrow escapes, but unfortunately he seems to bear a charmed life. His letters are full of details, and I wonder he gets them past the Field Censorship, but I suppose he censors his own.

She laughs at them and calls them her Colonel's dispatches; she says he is so accustomed to writing official reports that the poor old man can't write an ordinary letter.

I told her that I thought the way he mentioned regiments and dispositions rather indiscreet, and she agrees, but she says he has asked her to keep them, with a view to forming a collection of letters written from the front whilst the incidents he describes are vivid in his mind. I suppose the old ass knows his own business, and one day the collection may be completed by a telegram "Regretting to announce, etc. etc." The sooner the better.

So the days passed pleasantly enough, and never by a gesture or word of mouth did she show that I was more to her than any other pleasant young man.

I kissed her when I arrived, I kissed her when I left, each day was the same. She would put her arms round my neck and look long and deeply into my eyes, then she would gently kiss my lips. Not an atom of emotion! not a spark from the fires which I feel must be raging beneath that diabolically[6] extraordinary[6] amazingly calm exterior.

On ordinary subjects she would chatter vivaciously enough and she can talk in a fascinating manner on every subject I care to bring up, but

---

6   These words are crossed out.—ETIENNE.

as soon as I drew the conversation round to a personal line she gradually became more silent and a far-away and distant look came into those wonderful eyes.

I have found out nothing about her beyond the fact that she has travelled all over Europe. I don't even know how old she is, but I should guess twenty-six.

I tried to find out a few details by means of discreet remarks at the Club and elsewhere.

She simply arrived here about a year ago—as a singer, and met the Colonel—beyond that, all is mystery. Everything about her attracts me powerfully, and this mystery adds subtleties to her charms.

This afternoon I went to say good-bye; I told her we were leaving "shortly," and she gently reproved me for disobeying the order which forbids discussion of movements, but I could see she was not greatly displeased.

After tea she played to me, music of the modern Russian school—Arensky, Sibelius and Pilsuki; a storm was brewing and we both felt sad.

She played for an hour or so, and then came and sat by me on a low divan by the fire. We were silent for a long while in the gathering gloom, whilst a thousand thoughts chased each other swiftly through my brain, as I endeavoured to summon up courage to say what I had determined I must say before I left her, perhaps for ever.

At last, when only her profile was visible against the glow of the logs, I spoke.

I told her quietly, calmly and almost dispassionately that I had grown to love her and that to me she was life itself. I told her that I had tried not to speak until I could endure no longer.

She sat very still as I spoke, and when I had finished there was a long silence and I gently stretched out my hand and stroked her lovely black hair. At last she rose and with averted face walked across the room, and stood looking at the storm through the big bow windows. I watched her, but did not dare follow.

At length she returned to me, and I saw what I had instinctively known the whole time—that she had been crying. I could not think why.

She put her arms round my neck, kissed me on the forehead and murmured, "Poor Karl."

I felt crushed; I dared not move for fear of breaking the magic of the moment, yet I longed to know more; I felt overwhelmed by some colossal mystery that seemed to be enveloping me in its folds. Why did she pity me? Why did she weep? Why didn't she answer my avowal? Why didn't she tell me something? Such were some of the problems that perplexed me.

It was thus when the clock chimed seven. I told her that my leave was up at seven o'clock, and that at 7.15 I had to be back on board the boat. She remembered this, and in an instant the past quarter of an hour might never have existed. She was all agitation and nervousness lest I should be late on board—though at the moment I would have cheerfully missed the boat to hear her say she loved me.

I tried to protest, but in vain. With feminine quickness she utilized the incident to avoid a situation she evidently found full of difficulty, and at 7.10, with the memory of a light kiss on my lips and her God-speed in my ears I was in a taxi driving to the docks in a blinding rain-storm—and we sail to-night.

For five, six, seven, perhaps ten days at the least, and at the most for ever, I am doomed to be away from her and without news of her. And I don't even know whether she loves me!

I think I can say she cares for me up to a certain point, but I want more.

> "Oh Zoe! of the violet eyes,
> And hair of blackest night
> Thy lips are brightest crimson,
> Thy skin is dazzling white.

"Oh! lay your head upon my breast,
And lift your lips to mine;
Then murmur in soft breathings,
Drink deep from what is thine.

"Then let the war rage onward,
Let kingdoms rise and fall;
To each shall be the other,
Their life, their hope, their all."[7]

At sea.

We are bound for the same old spot as last time.

Alten must have been drinking like a fish lately; his breath smells like a distillery; he is apparently partial to schnapps, which he gets easily in Bruges.

I can't help admiring the man, as he is a rigid teetotaller at sea, though he must find the strain well nigh intolerable, judging from the condition he was in when he came on board last night. He was really totally unfit to take charge of the boat, and I virtually took her down the canal, though with sottish obstinacy he insisted on remaining on the bridge.

This morning, though his complexion was a hideous yellow colour, he seems quite all right. I shall play a little trick on him at dinner to-night.

I have begun to get to know some of the crew by now; they are a fine lot of youngsters with a seasoning of half a dozen older men. The coxswain, Schmitt by name, is a splendid old petty officer who has been in the U-boat service since 1911.

His favourite enjoyment is to spin yarns to the younger members of the crew, who know of his weakness and play up to it.

He has a favourite expression which runs thus:

---

7 I am indebted to Commander C. C. for the above rough translation of Karl's effusion.—ETIENNE.

"His Majesty the Kaiser said Germany's future lies on the sea; I say Germany's future lies under the sea."

He is inordinately fond of this statement, and the youngsters continually say: "What made you take to U-boat work, Schmitt?" and the invariable reply is as above. When he has been asked the question about half a dozen times in the course of a day, he is liable to become suspicious, and if his questioner is within range Schmitt stares at him for a few seconds in an absent-minded way, then an arm like that of a gorilla shoots out, and the quizzer *(Untersucher)* receives a resounding box on the ears to the huge delight of his companions. The old man then permits his iron-lipped mouth to relax into a caustic smile, after which he is left in peace for some time.

At the wheel he is an artist, for he seems to divine what the next order is going to be, or if he is steering her on a course he predicts the direction of the next wave even as a skilful chess player works out the moves ahead.

* * * * *

I am rather weary and ought to go to bed, but before I lose the savour I must record the splendid fun I had with Alten at dinner.

We were dining alone, as the navigator was on the bridge, and the engineer was busy with a slight leak in the cooking water service. I have said that, though a heavy drinker by nature, Alten is a strict abstainer at sea. Accordingly I produced a small flask of rum, half-way through dinner, and helped myself to a liberal tot, placing the liquor between us on the table. As the sight met his eyes and the aroma greeted his nostrils, a gleam of joy flashed across his face, to be succeeded by a frown.

With an amiable smile I proffered the flask to him, remarking at the same time: "You don't drink at sea, do you?"

In a thick voice he muttered, "No! Yes—no! thank you."

With an air of having noticed nothing, I resumed my meal, but out of the corner of my eye I watched his left hand on the table near the flask. It was most interesting, all the veins stood out like ropes, and his knuckles almost burst through the skin.

This went on for about thirty seconds, when he choked out something about needing a breath of fresh air. As he got up his face was brick red, and I almost thought he'd have a fit.

Whether by accident or design he pulled the cloth as he got out from between the settee and the table and upset the flask.

He was apparently incapable of apologizing, for he rushed up on deck.

A few minutes later the navigating officer came down and asked what was up?

I said: "What do you mean?"

He said: "Well, the Captain came up just now, swearing like a trooper, and told me to get to the devil out of it; it didn't seem advisable to question him, so I got out of it and came down."

I expressed my opinion that the Captain must be feeling sea-sick and was ashamed to say so. I also suggested to the navigator that he should take the Captain a little brandy in case he was not feeling well, but the navigator declared he was going to stay down in the warmth till he was sent for. Alten is a great coarse brute. Fancy allowing a material substance such as alcohol to grip one's mentality.

Thank Heaven I have nerves of iron; nothing would affect me!

And now to bed, though I must just read my account of our day in the forest. Darling girl, may I dream of thee.

* * * * *

We laid our mines without trouble at 5 a.m. this morning, though at midnight we had a most unpleasant experience.

I was asleep, as it was my morning watch, when I was awakened by the harsh rattle of the diving alarms.

The Diesel subsided with a few spasmodic coughs into silence, and as I jumped out of my bunk and groped for my short sea boots, the navigator and helmsman came tumbling down the conning tower, with the navigator shouting, "Take her down," as hard as you like.

The men at the planes had them "hard-to-dive" in an instant.

The vents had been opened as the hooters sounded, and Alten, who had jumped into the control room, immediately rang down, "All out on the electric motors."

In thirty seconds from the original alarm we were at an angle of twenty degrees down by the bow, and I had sat down heavily on the battery boards, completely surprised by the sudden tilt of the deck.

It occurred to me that the air was escaping through the vents with a strangely loud noise, but before I could consider the matter further or even inquire the reason for this sudden dive, the noise increased to a terrifying extent, and whilst I prepared myself for the worst it culminated into a roar as of fifty express trains going through a tunnel, mingled with the noise of a high-powered aeroplane engine.

The roar drummed and beat and shook the boat, then died away as suddenly as it came; a moment later there was a severe jar. We had struck the bottom, still maintaining our angle.

I painfully got to my feet and then discovered from the navigator that he had suddenly seen two white patches of foam 800 yards on the starboard bow, which resolved themselves into the bow waves of a destroyer approaching at full speed to ram.

We had dived just in time, and her knife-edged bow, driven by 30,000 horse power, had slid through the water a very few feet above our conning tower.

Luckily he had not dropped any depth charges. We were not, however, completely free of our troubles, though we had cheated the destroyer.

Examination of the chart, showed the bottom to be mud, and on attempting to move the foremost hydroplanes, the plane motor fuses blew out. This showed that the boat was buried in the mud right up to her foremost planes, which were immovable.

The hydrophone watchkeeper reported that he could still hear fast-running propellers, though probably some distance away, and as this showed that our old enemy was still nosing about we were very anxious not to break surface. We just blew "A."[8] At least we started to blow "A," but Alten wisely decided that, as it was a calm night with a half-moon, the bubbles on the surface might be rather conspicuous, so we stopped the blow and put the pump on. We also flooded "W".[9] This had no effect on her at all.

We then pumped out "Q" and "P," leaving "W" full, and adjusted our trim to give her only three tons negative buoyancy, just enough to keep us on the bottom if she came out of the mud.

In this position we went full speed astern on the motors, 1,500 amps on each, and all the crew in the after-compartment. No result. We then pumped the outer diving tanks on the port side to give her a list to starboard. Still she remained fixed.

So at 2 a.m. we decided to risk it and we put a slow blow on all tanks.

When she had about fifty tons positive buoyancy she suddenly bucketed up, and, as the motors were running full speed astern at the time, we came up and broke surface stern first. In a few seconds we were trimmed down again, and as a precautionary measure we proceeded for a couple of miles at twenty metres, when, coming up to periscope depth, we surfaced, and finding all clear we proceeded. We were put down by a trawler at dawn, though she never saw us. After half an hour's hanging about she moved off, which was lucky, as she was right on our billet.

---

8 Probably their foremost internal tank.—ETIENNE.]
9 Presumably their after internal tank.—ETIENNE.

We are now proceeding to a spot somewhat to the eastward of Cape St. Abbs,[10] as we have instructions to do a two-days patrol here and sink shipping.

We ought to start business to-morrow morning.

* * * * *

We should be in to-night, then for my little Zoe!

But I must record what we have done. Already I am getting much pleasure from reading my diary. Strange how it amuses one to see little bits of oneself on paper, and the less garnished and franker the truths the more entertaining it is.

"The torpedo had jumped clean out of the water a hundred yards short of the steamer and had then dived under her."

---
10 St. Abbs Head.—ETIENNE

"We were put down by a trawler at dawn."

A moment later there was a severe jar; we had struck the bottom

The hours here are so long and boring at times that I feel I want to talk intimately with someone. Failing Zoe I turn to my notebooks.

The first steamer we sighted raised high hopes, at least her smoke did, for we saw enough smoke on the horizon to make us think we were to see the Grand Fleet, and we promptly dived. We cruised towards her for about half an hour, and then hung about where we were, as we found that her course would take the ship close to us.

As the situation developed, Alten, who was up in the conning tower at the "A" periscope, gave us a certain amount of information, and we gathered that all this smoke was pouring out of the pipe-stem tunnel of a wretched little English tramp.

I found it most irritating, standing in the control room (my action station) and not knowing what was going on.

There is only one good job in a submarine and that is the Captain's. He knows and decides everything. The rest of us are in his hands and take things on trust. I object on principle to my life being held in Alten's hands. It is all very well for the crew, for, to start with, they have no imagination, and to most of them their mental horizon stops at the walls of the boat. Secondly, they have the consolation of mechanical activities; they make and break switches and open and close valves—they work with their hands. An officer has imagination, and only works with his head.

As we attacked the steamer, all one heard was murmurs from Alten, such as: "Raise!" "Lower!" "Take her down to ten metres!" "Half speed!" "Slow!" "Bring her up to five metres!" "Raise!" "Lower!"

I endeavoured to simulate an air of unconcern which I was far from feeling.

Not that I was a prey to physical fear; I flatter myself it is so far unknown to me, and there was no great danger, but simply that I longed to know what was happening. At length I heard the welcome order:

"Starboard tube. Stand by!"

Which was followed almost immediately by the order: "Fire!"

There was a kind of coughing grunt, and the starboard torpedo proceeded on its errand of destruction.

Every ear was strained for the sound of the explosion, but all we were vouchsafed was a torrent of blasphemy from Alten.

The torpedo had jumped clean out of the water a hundred yards short of the steamer, and had then evidently dived under the ship; so I gathered later when Alten had calmed down somewhat. We were about to surface and give her the gun, when luckily Alten took a good sweep round with the skyscraper and discovered one of those wretched little airships about a mile away, coming towards the steamer, which was wailing piteously, on her syren.

As the chart showed forty metres we decided to bottom and have lunch.

Over lunch we discussed the misadventure. Alten was loud in his curses of Tanzerman (the torpedo lieutenant at Bruges), from whom he had got the torpedo in guaranteed good condition only forty-eight hours before we sailed. He launched forth into a tirade against the torpedo staff at Bruges, and, warming to his subject, he roundly abused the whole of the depot personnel, whom he stigmatized as a set of hard-drinking, shore-loafing ruffians, who were incapable of realizing that they existed for the benefit of the boats' personnel and "material."

I naturally disagreed, and did so the more readily that I conscientiously disagree with him. I find that there is a tendency on the part of some of these submarine officers, who have been U-boating a long time, to get into narrow grooves. Most reserve officers are not like this, as they have only been in during the war. Alten is an exception; he left the Hamburg-Amerika on two years' half pay in 1912, and was, of course, kept on in 1914. After all, the depot staff are Germans, and as such labour for the Fatherland, and though their work in office and workshop is not so dangerous as ours, on the other hand they have not got the stimulation before their eyes, of glory to be gained. Personally I am of the opinion that the torpedo broke surface because, being fired from the outside tubes, it probably started too shallow, dived deep, recovered shallow and dived deep, broke surface and dived very deep. A sticky motor or sluggish weight would give this effect.

And are these external tubes water-tight? Theoretically, yes, but what of practice? We have been down to forty metres several times during this trip, and not once have we had a chance on the surface of getting at the two external tubes; add to which our depth gear, with the pivots of the weight exposed to water if the tube does flood and then you have rust, corrosion and heaven knows what complications.

I saw a British Mark 11.50 torpedo at the torpedo shop at Bruges the other day, and I was much struck with their deep depth gear, which is of the unrestrained Uhlan type, i.e., weight and valve interdependent. But then the main feature is that the whole gear is contained in a separate water-tight chamber.

Our system is certainly a great saving in space, and is much neater in design, whilst I prefer the Uhlan principle of valve conjuncting with weight, but it would be interesting to know whether the British have much trouble with the depth-keeping of their torpedo.

I have written quite a disquisition on depth gears; I must get on with my record of events.

After lunch we had a good look round, but the small airship was still hanging about, flying slowly in large circles.

We were rather surprised to meet one of these despicable little sausages or "Zeppelin's Spawn," as the navigator calls them, so far from land, and at dark we surfaced and proceeded on one engine on an easterly course, charging the battery right up with the other engine.

Dawn revealed a blank horizon, not a vestige of mast, funnel or smoke in sight.

We ambled along in fine though cold weather, and I took advantage of the peacefulness of everything to do a really good series of Müller on the upper deck, stripped to the waist, and allowed the keen air to play its invigorating currents on my torso.

Alten silently watched me from the conning tower, with a sneering expression on his face. The navigator, who is quite a decent youngster, though of no family, was, I could plainly see, struck by my development, and asked to be initiated into the series of exercises. I agreed willingly enough to show them to him. I will confess I wish Zoe could have seen me as I perspired with healthy exercise.

At about 11 a.m. a couple of masts, then two more, then another, appeared above the horizon. The visibility was extreme, so we at once dived and proceeded at full speed, ten metres.

We had been going thus for perhaps half an hour when Alten remarked that he would have another look at the convoy. We eased speed, came up to six metres, and Alten proceeded up into the conning tower to use "A" periscope.

He had hardly applied his eye to the lens when he sharply ordered the boat to ten metres, accompanying this order with another to the motor room demanding utmost speed *(Ausserste Kraft)*. I went up to the conning tower and found him white with excitement.

"Look!" he exclaimed, pointing to the periscope, entirely forgetful of the fact that we were at ten metres. I looked, and of course saw nothing; furious at the trick I considered he had played on me I turned on him, to be disarmed by his apology.

"Sorry! I forgot! The whole British battle cruiser force is there."

It was now my turn to be excited, and I rushed down to the motor room determined to give her every amp she would take. The port foremost motor was sparking like the devil, rings of cursed sparks shooting round the commutator, but this was no time for ceremony. I relentlessly ordered the field current to be still further reduced.

We were actually running with an F.C. of 3.75 amps,[11] for a period, when the sparking assumed the appearance of a ring of fire and, fearing a commutator strip would melt, I ordered an F.C. of five amps.

We thus passed a quarter of an hour full of strain, the tension of which was reflected in the attitude of all the men. Alten had announced his

---

11 The lower the field current the faster the motor goes. 3.75 is almost incredibly low for a motor of this type—at least according to British practice.—ETIENNE.

intention of using the stern torpedo tube after his failure in the morning, and the crew of this tube were crouched at their stations like a gun's crew in the last few seconds preparatory to opening fire. The switchboard attendants gripped the regulating rheostatts as if by their personal efforts they could urge the boat on faster. Old Schmitt, at the helm, never lifted his eyes from the compass repeater.

At length: "Slow both!" "Bring her to six metres!" came from the conning tower, to which place I proceeded to hear the news.

Slowly the periscope was raised and I held my breath; a groan came from Alten and he turned away. For a fraction of a second I was almost pleased at his obvious pain, then, sick with disappointment, I took his place.

Yes! it was all over. There they were, and with hungry eyes and depressed heart I saw five great battle cruisers, of which I recognized the *Tiger* with her three great funnels, the *Princess Royal*, *Lion* and two others, zigzagging along at 25 knots, at a distance of 12,000 metres, across our bow.

They were surrounded by a numerous screen of destroyers and light cruisers, the former at that range through the periscope appearing as black smudges.

It is not often one is permitted such a spectacle in modern war, and I could not tear myself away from the sight of those great brutes, whom I had fought when in the *Derflingger* at Dogger Bank and again when in the *König* at Jutland. So near and yet so far, and as they rapidly drew away so did all the visions of an Iron Cross. As soon as they were out of sight, we surfaced in order to report what we had seen to Zeebrugge and Heligoland.

Everything seemed against us. I had gone on the bridge with the navigator; Alten, with a face as black as hell, had gone to the wardroom. About ten minutes elapsed when I heard a fearful altercation going on below. I stepped down to find the young wireless operator trembling in front of Alten, who was overwhelming him with a flood of abuse.

As I reached the wardroom, Alten shook his fist in the man's face and bellowed:

"Make the d—thing work, I tell you."

"Impossible, Captain, the main condenser—" the man began.

Purple with rage, Alten seized a heavy pair of parallel rulers, and before I could check him hurled them full in the operator's face. Bleeding copiously, the youth fell to the deck in a stunned condition.

It was then, for the first time, that I noticed a half-empty bottle of spirits on the table, which colossal quantity he must have consumed in about a quarter of an hour.

Turning to me, this semi-madman pointed to the wireless operator with his foot and growled:

"Have him removed."

This I did, and then, lowering the periscope, I ordered the boat to fifteen metres. We proceeded at this depth until 8 p.m., when I was informed that the Captain was in his bunk and wished to see me.

I discovered him with his face to the ship's side, and upon my reporting myself he ordered me, firstly to throw that blasted bottle overboard (an unnecessary proceeding, as it was empty), and secondly to surface and shape course for Zeebrugge.

At midnight he relieved me, apparently perfectly normal.

The wireless operator has been laid up all day and has a nasty cut on the head. The navigator, a great scandal-monger, has heard from the engineer that Alten was speaking to him alone this morning, and the engineer believes that Alten has given him five hundred marks to say he fell down a hatch.

Hooray! Blankenberg buoy has just been reported in sight! Soon I shall see my Zoe!

* * * * *

With what high hopes did I write the last few lines a few hours ago, and how they were dashed to the ground, for on going into the Mess at Bruges I found amongst my letters a note from her, which was terrible in its brevity. She simply said:

"DEAR KARL,
"I am going away for some days, and as I shall be travelling it is no good giving you an address. To our next meeting!

"ZOE."

How horribly vague; not an indication of her destination, her object, or the probable length of her absence. Of course I rushed round to the flat, but found the place shut up. The porter told me she had gone away with her maid. He couldn't say when she'd be back—if at all! I gave him ten marks, and he said she might be away a fortnight. If I'd given him twenty he'd have said a week; he obviously didn't know.

I feel I could do anything to-night; any mad, evil thing would appeal to me.

There is a most fearful uproar coming from the guest-room, where a large and rowdy party are entertaining the chorus of a travelling *revue* company. I saw them when they arrived, horribly common-looking women, with legs like mine tubes.

* * * * *

Another day and still no news; I don't know how I shall stick it. She might have had the softness of heart to write to me. She knows my address.

This evening a letter from the little mother, who asks whether I can find time to go to Frankfurt when I have leave; at the end of the letter she mentions that Rosa has joined the Women's Voluntary Auxiliary

Corps of Army Nurses. I suppose she thought she'd like her photograph taken in some fancy uniform as "Rosa Freinland, one of our Frankfurt beauties, now on war work!" Holding the patient's hand is about the only work she intends doing.

Women as a class are the same the world over. We are well supplied with English papers in the Mess here; they come regularly from Amsterdam, and in their pages I see, just as in ours, pictures of the Countess this and the Lord that, photographed in becoming attitudes doing war work. It seems agricultural pursuits are the fashion in England at present—wait till our U-boat war gets its knife well into their fat guts, it will be more than fashionable to work in the fields then.

The British Empire is undeniably a great creation, or rather not so much a creation as a thing arrived at accidentally, but it lacks solidarity. It sprawls, a confused mass of races and creeds, around the world. Its very immensity lays it open to attack, it has a dozen Achilles heels from Ireland to Egypt and South Africa to India.

I met a man only yesterday who was recently at the propaganda department of the Foreign Office, and without going into details he gave me a very good idea of the good work that is going on in Britain's canker spots.

Ireland is considered particularly promising to those in the know.

Now for an agitated night! To think that a girl should disturb me so!

* * * * *

Two days have passed, or, rather, dragged their interminable lengths away, for there is still not a vestige of news. I have been twice to the flat with no result, except to receive a piece of impertinence from the porter the last time I was there.

No news.

* * * * *

Still no news, and we sail in forty-eight hours.

At sea, off the Isle of Wight.

It is some days since I turned for solace and enjoyment, amidst the discomforts of this life, to my pen and notebook.

What strange tricks fate plays with us, and how lucky it is that one cannot foresee the future.

Here I am in U.39—but I must start at the beginning. My last entry was the depressing one of still no news. Well, I have had news, but it was like a drop of water in the mouth of a parched-up man. Another agonizing twenty-four hours passed, and I was sitting in my room about ten o'clock, trying to resign myself to the idea that the next night I should be starting out for my third trip without news of her, when the telephone bell rang. I lifted the receiver and to my amazed joy heard a voice that I could have recognized in a thousand. It was Zoe!

I was quite incapable of any remark, and my confusion was further increased when, after a few "Hello's," which I idiotically repeated, her clear, level tones said: "Is that you, Karl? How are you?" How was I? What a question to ask! I wanted to tell her that I was bubbling with joy, that a thousand-kilogramme load had been lifted from my chest, that my blood was coursing through my veins, that I, usually so cool, was trembling with excitement, that I could have kissed the mouthpiece of the humble instrument that linked us together. Yet I was quite incapable of answering her simple question! I can't imagine what I expected her to say, for upon reflection her remark was a very ordinary one, and indeed under the circumstances quite natural, but, as I say, in actual fact I was tongue-tied.

I suppose I must have said something, for I next remember her saying: "Well, you might ask how I am;" and to my horror I realized that she thought I was being rude!

My abject apologies were cut short by her tantalizing laugh, and I understood that the adorable one was teasing me. When at length I made myself believe that I really was talking to this most elusive and delightful woman I wasted no time in suggesting that, late though it was, I might be permitted to go round and see her. She would not permit this, as she said it would create grave scandal, and the Colonel might hear about it upon his return. I pleaded hard and urged my departure in twenty-four hours.

She was firm and reproved me for discussing movements over the telephone. She was right; I was a fool to do so; but Zoe destroys all my caution. However, she said that I might lunch with her next day, and that she had some new music to play to me. I ventured to ask where she had been, but this question was plainly unpleasing to my lady, so I dropped the subject. I blew her a goodnight kiss over the telephone, to which I think I caught an answer, and then she rang off.

Ten minutes had not elapsed, when a messenger entered and informed me that I was wanted at the Commodore's office at once.

A strange feeling of uneasiness and that of impending misfortune overcame me. I felt like a naughty school-boy about to interview the headmaster.

I followed the messenger into the Commodore's office, and found myself alone with the great man. He was seated at a huge roll-top desk, which was the only article of furniture in a room which was to all intents and purposes papered with large scale charts of the east and south coasts of England and of the Channel and North Sea.

The Commodore was sealing an envelope as I came in; he looked up and saw me, then, without taking any further notice of me, he resumed his business with the envelope. I felt that I was in the presence of a personality, and I was, for "Old Man Max" is one of the ten men who count in the Naval Administration. He had a reading lamp on his desk, and I remember noticing that the light shining through its green shade imparted a yellow parchment-like effect to the top of his old bald head. With dainty care he finished sealing the envelope, then, picking up a telephone transmitter, he snapped "Admiralty!" In about a minute he was connected, and to my astonishment I realized that he was talking to the duty captain of the operations department in Berlin.

His words chilled my heart, for he said: "Commodore speaking! U.39 sails at 2 a.m. for operation F.Q.H.—Repeat."

His words were apparently repeated to his satisfaction, for while I was vainly endeavouring to convince myself that I was unconnected with the sailing of U.39, he banged the receiver into place (Old Man Max does everything in bangs) and snapped at me.

"You Lieutenant Von Schenk?"

I admitted I was, and then heard this disgusting news.

"Kranz, 1st Lieutenant U.39, reported suddenly ill, Zeebrugge, poisoning—you relieve him. Ship sails in one hour forty minutes from now—my car leaves here in forty minutes and takes you to Zeebrugge. Here are operation orders—inform Von Weissman he acknowledges receipt direct to me on 'phone. That's all."

He handed me the envelope and I suppose I walked outside—at least I found myself in the corridor turning the confounded envelope round and round. For one mad moment I felt like rushing in and saying: "But, sir, you don't understand I'm lunching with Zoe to-morrow!"

Then the mental picture which this idea conjured up made me shake with suppressed laughter and I remembered that war was war and that I had only thirty-five minutes in which to collect such gear as I had handy— most of my sea things being in U.C.47—and say goodbye to Zoe.

I ran to my room and made the corridors echo with shouts for my faithful Adolf. The excellent man was soon on the scene, and whilst he stuffed underclothing, towels and other necessary gear into a bag he had purloined from someone's room, I rang up Zoe. I wasted ten minutes getting through, but at last I heard a deliciously sleepy voice murmur, "Who's that?"

I told her, and added that I was off; to my secret joy, an intensely disappointed and long-drawn "Oooh!" came over the wire. So she does care a bit, I thought. Mad ideas of pretending to be suddenly ill crossed my mind—anything to gain twenty-four hours—but the Fatherland is above all such considerations, and after some pleasant talk and many wishes of good luck from the darling girl, with a heavy heart I bade her good-night.

The Old Man's car, which is a sixty horse-power Benz, was waiting at the Mess entrance, and once clear of the sentries we raced down the flat, well-metalled road to Zeebrugge in a very short time. The guard at Bruges barrier had 'phoned us through to the Zeebrugge fortified zone, and we were admitted without delay. In three-quarters of an hour from my interview with old Max I was scrambling across a row of U-boats to reach my new ship, U.39.

I went down the after hatch, reported myself to Von Weissman and delivered his orders to him, of which he acknowledged receipt direct to the Commodore according to instructions. Von Weissman is a very different stamp of man to Alten; of medium height, he has sandy-coloured hair, steel-grey eyes and a protruding jaw. He is what he looks, a fine North Prussian, and is, of course, of excellent family, as the Weissmans have been settled in Grinetz for a long period.

He struck me as being about thirty years of age, and on his heart he wore the Cross of the second class. I have heard of him before as being well in the running towards an *ordre pour le mérite*.

An interesting chart is hanging in the wardroom, on which is marked the last resting-place of every ship he has sunk. He puts a coloured dot, the tint of which varies with the tonnage, black up to 2,000, blue from 2,000-5,000, brown 5,000-8,000, green 8,000-11,000, and a red spot with the ship's name for anything over 11,000. He has got about 120,000 tons at present. He opposes the Arnauld de la Perrière school of thought, which pins faith on the gun, and Weissman has done nearly all his work with the good old torpedo.

Altogether, undoubtedly a man to serve with.

The U.39 was in that buzzing and semi-active condition which to a trained eye is a sure indication that the ship is about to sail. Punctually at five minutes to 2 a.m. Weissman went to the bridge, and at 2 a.m. the wires were slipped and we started on a ten days' trip. As the dim lights on the mole disappeared and the ceaseless fountain of star-shells, mingling with the flashing of guns, rose inland on our port beam my mind travelled overland to the flat at Bruges, and I wondered whether Zoe was lying awake listening to the ceaseless rumble of the Flanders cannon. We went on at full speed, as it was our intention to pass the Dover Straits before dawn. Though our intelligence bureau issues the most alarming reports as to the frightfulness of the defences here I was agreeably surprised at the ease with which we passed. Von Weissman, to whom I had hinted that we might find the passage tricky, rather laughed at my suggestion, and described to me his method, which, at all events, has the merit of simplicity.

He always goes through with the tide, so as to take as short a time as possible, and he always decides on a course and steers it as closely as possible, keeping to the surface unless he sights anything, and diving as soon as anything shows up. Even if he dives he goes on as fast as possible on his course, irrespective of whether he is being bombed or not.

I must say it worked very well last night. We shaped a course to pass five miles west of Gris Nez, and when that light, which for some reason the French had commodiously lit that night, was abeam, we sighted a black object, probably a trawler or destroyer, about half a dozen miles away right ahead. Weissman immediately dived and, without deviating a degree from his course, held on at three-quarters speed on the motors. Some time later the hydrophone watchkeeper reported the sound of propellers in his listeners, and that he judged them to be close at hand, so I imagine we passed very nearly directly underneath whatever it was.

After an hour's submerging we rose, and found dawn breaking over a leaden and choppy sea. Nothing being in sight, we continued on the surface for an hour, charging batteries with the starboard engine (500 amps on each), but at 9 a.m., the clouds lying low and an aerial patrol being frequent hereabouts, we dived and cruised steadily down channel at slow speed, keeping periscope depth.

Several times in the course of the forenoon we sighted small destroyers and convoy craft[12] in the distance, all steering westerly. They were probably returning from escorting troopships over to France last night. In every case we went to sixty feet long before they could have seen our "stick."[13] Weissman is evidently as cautious in this matter as he is hardy in others; the more I see of him the more I like him; he is a man of breeding, and it is of value to serve in this boat.

As I write we are on the surface about ten miles east of the Isle of Wight, still steering down channel. To-night at midnight we report our position to Zeebrugge, up till now we have maintained wireless silence for fear of the British and French directional stations picking up our signals and fixing our position.

After supper this evening Von Weissman explained to me the general plan of our operations for the next eight days. Our cruising billet is about 150 miles south-west of the Scillys, at the focal point where trade for Liverpool and Bristol and the up-channel trade diverges. Von Weissman says that this is a plum billet and we should do well.

I feel this is going to be better than those piffling little mine-laying trips, and though we shall be away ten days, it will qualify me for four days' leave in Belgium.

* * * * *

There was nearly an awkward moment last night, or, rather, there was an awkward moment, and nearly an awkward accident. I relieved the navigator at midnight (the pilot is an unassuming individual called Siegel) and took on the middle watch. It was blowing about force 4 from the south-west, and a nasty short, lumpy sea was running which caught us

---

12 Probably "P" boats.—ETIENNE.
13 Periscope.—ETIENNE.

just on the port bow. About once every ten seconds she missed her step with the waves and, dipping her nose into it, shovelled up tons of water, which, as the bow lifted, raced aft and, breaking against the gun, flung itself in clouds of spray against the bridge. In a very few minutes every exposed portion of me was streaming with water.

At about 2 a.m. I had turned my back to the sea for a moment, and my thoughts were for an instant in Bruges, when, on facing forward once again I saw a sight which effectually brought me back to earth.

This was the spectacle of two black shapes, evidently steamers, one on either bow, distant, I should estimate, 600 or 700 metres. I had to make a quick decision, and I decided that to fire a torpedo in that sea with any hope of a hit, especially with the boat on surface, was useless; furthermore, that at any moment either of the steamers might sight us from their high bridge and turn and ram.

These thoughts were the work of an instant, and I at once rang the diving bell, and, pushing the look-out before me, in five seconds I was in the conning tower and had the hatch down. I at once proceeded down into the boat, and the first thing that struck my eye was the diving gauge with the needle practically stationary at two metres.

The boat was not going down properly! and for an instant I was rudely shaken, until a cool voice from the wardroom remarked, "Helm hard a-port," an order that was instantly obeyed, and as she began to turn the moving needle on the depth gauge began its journey round the dial. It was the Captain who had spoken. As soon as he heard the diving alarm he was out of his bunk, and a glance at the gauge he has fitted in the wardroom told him we were not sinking rapidly. In an instant he had put his finger on the trouble, which was that we were almost head on to the sea, with the result that he had given the order as stated above, which, bringing us beam on to the sea, had caused her to dive with ease. He is efficiency itself!

As I explained to him what had happened, the noise of propellers at varying distances from us overhead led him to state his belief that we had run into a convoy homeward bound to Southampton from the Atlantic.

He approved of my actions in every particular, save only in my omission to bring the boat away from the sea as I began to dive.

This morning we are beginning to get the full force of what is evidently going to be a south-westerly gale of some violence. The seas are getting larger as we debouch into the Atlantic. This looks bad for business.

* * * * *

At the moment we are practically hove to on the surface, with the port engine just jogging to keep her head on to sea and the starboard ticking round to give her a long, slow charge of 200 amps.

The wind is force 7-8 and a very big sea is running which makes it entirely impossible to open the conning tower hatch; the engine is getting its air through the special mushroom ventilator, which is apparently not designed to supply both the boat's requirements and those of the engine; the whole ventilator gets covered with sea every now and then, during which period until the baffle drains get the water away no air can get in, so the engine has a good suck at the air in the boat, the result of all this being a slight vacuum in the boat. It is a very unpleasant sensation, and made me very sick. This is really a form of sickness due to the rarefied air.

I had a great surprise when I looked at the barograph this morning as the needle had gone right off the paper at the bottom, and at first glance I thought we had struck a tropical depression of the first magnitude, which, flouting all the laws of meteorology, had somehow found its way to the English Channel; but the engineer explained to me that, as I have already stated, the low atmospheric pressure in the boat was due to the conning-tower hatch being shut down.

"As the dim lights on the mole disappeared, the ceaseless fountain of starshells mingling with the flashing of guns, rose inland on our port beam."

"We hit her aft for the second time."

I have discovered that Von Weissman is a martyr to sea-sickness—all day he has been lying down as white as a sheet and subsisting on milk tablets and sips of brandy; yet such is the man's inflexibility of will that he forces himself to make a tour of inspection right round the boat every six hours, night and day. It is this will to conquer which has made Germans unconquerable, though "Come the four corners of the world in arms" against us, as the great poet says.

We are, of course, keeping watch from inside the conning tower; it is, at all events, dry, but as to seeing anything one might as well be looking out through a small glass window from inside a breakwater! To bed till 4 a.m.

* * * * *

A most unprofitable day. I grudge every day away from Zoe on which we do nothing. This morning about noon the gale blew itself out, but a heavy confused sea continued to run.

At 2 p.m. we saw a most tantalizing spectacle. A big tank steamer, fully 600 feet long and of probably 17,000 tons burthen hove in sight, escorted by two destroyers. To attack with the gun was impossible, as we could only keep the conning tower open when stern to sea, and in any case the two destroyers prevented any surface work. We tried to get in for an attack, but we had not seen her in time, and the best we could do was to get within 3,000 yards, at which range it would have been absurd to have wasted a torpedo, the chances of hitting being 100 to 1 against, even if the torpedo had run properly in the sea that was on.

I had a good look at her through the foremost periscope in between the waves, and it maddened me to see all that oil, doubtless from Tampico for the Grand Fleet, going safely by. The destroyers were having a bad time of it, crashing into the sea like porpoises, their funnels white with salt, and their bridges enveloped in sheets of water and spray. They little thought that, barely a mile away, amidst the tumbling, crested waves a German eye was watching them!

There is no doubt these damned British have pluck, for it was the last sort of weather in which one would have expected to find destroyers at sea, and yet I suppose they do this throughout the winter.

After all, one would expect them to be tough fellows—they are of Teutonic stock—though by their bearing one might imagine that the Creator made an Englishman and then Adam.

Let's hope we get some decent weather to-morrow. I have just been refreshing my memory by reading of what I wrote in the book, concerning the day in the forest with the adorable girl. There is an exquisite pleasure in transporting the mind into such memories of the past when the body is in such surroundings as the present, if only I could will myself to dream of her!

* * * * *

A fine day in every sense of the word. The weather has been and remains excellent, and I have been present at my first sinking. It was absurdly commonplace. At 10 a.m. this morning a column of smoke crept upwards from the southern horizon.

Von Weissman steered towards it on the surface until two masts and the top of a funnel appeared. We dived and proceeded slowly under water on a southerly course.

Half an hour passed and Von Weissman brought the boat up to periscope depth and had a look. He called to me to come and see, an invitation I accepted with alacrity.

With natural excitement I looked through the periscope and there she was, unconsciously ambling to her doom like a fat sheep.

She was a steamer (British) of about 4,000 tons, slugging home at a steady ten knots, but she was destined to come to her last mooring place ahead of schedule time!

We dipped our periscope and I went forward to the tubes. Five minutes elapsed and the order instrument bell rang, the pointer flicking to "Stand by." I personally removed the firing gear safety pin and put the repeat to "Ready." A breathless pause, then a slight shake and destruction was on its way, whilst I realized by the angle of the boat that Weissman was taking us down a few metres.

That shows his coolness, he didn't even trouble to watch his shot.

Anxiously I watch the second hand of my stop watch. Weissman had told me the range would be about 500 metres—30 seconds—31—32—33—has he missed?—34—35—3—A dull rumble comes through the water and the whole boat shakes. Hurra! we have hit, and the order "Surface" comes along the voice pipe.

The cheerful voice of the blower is heard, evacuating the tanks; I run to the conning tower and closely follow Weissman up the ladder. At last I am on the bridge. There she is! What a sight!

I feel that I shall never forget what she looked like, though, if all goes well, I shall see many another fine ship go to her grave.

But she was my first; I felt the same sensation when, as a boy, I shot my first roe-deer in the Black Forest, one instant a living thing beautiful to perfection, the next my rifle spoke and a bleeding carcase lay beneath the fine trees. So with this ship. I am a sailor, and to every sailor every ship that floats has, as it were, a soul, a personality, an entity; to carry the analogy further, a merchant craft is like some fat beast of utility, an ox, a cow, or a sheep, whilst a warship is a lion if she is a battleship, a leopard if she is a light cruiser, etc.; in all cases worthy game.

But War has little use for sentimentality! and in my usual wandering manner I see that I have meandered from the point and quite forgotten what she did look like.

What I saw was this:

I saw that the steamer had been hit forward on the starboard side. The upper portion of the stem piece was almost down to the water level, her foremost hold was obviously filling rapidly. Her stern was high out of water, the red ensign of England flapping impotently on the ensign staff. Her propeller, which was still slowly revolving, thrashed the water, and this heightened the impression that I was watching the struggles of a dying animal. The propeller was revolving in spasmodic jerks, due, I imagine, to the fast failing steam only forcing the cranks over their dead centres with an effort.

A boat was being lowered with haste from the two davits abreast the funnel on one side, but when she was full of men and, due to the angle of the ship, well down by the bow, someone inboard let go the foremost fall or else it broke, for the bows of the boat fell downwards and half a dozen figures were projected in grotesque attitudes into the sea. For a few seconds the boat swung backwards and forwards, like a pendulum.

When she came to rest, hanging vertically downwards from the stern, I noticed that a few men were still clinging like flies to her thwarts. Truly, anything is better than the Atlantic in winter. Meanwhile the ship had ceased to sink as far as outward signs went.

I mentioned this to Von Weissman, who was at my side with a slight smile on his face, amused doubtless at the eagerness with which I watched every detail of this, to me, novel tragedy. He answered me that I need not worry, that she was being supported by an air lock somewhere forward, that the water was slowly creeping into her and her boilers would probably soon go.

This remarkable man was absolutely correct.

There was an interval of about five minutes, during which another boat, evidently successfully lowered from the other side, came round her stern, picked up one or two men from the water and also collected the survivors in the hanging boat; then the steamer suddenly sank another two feet, there was a dull rumbling, as of heavy machinery falling from a height, a muffled report, a cloud of steam and smoke, a sucking noise and then a pool in the water, in the middle of which odd bits of wood and other buoyant debris kept on bobbing up. Nothing else!

No! I am wrong, there were two other things: a U-boat, representing the might of Germany, and a whaler with perhaps twenty men in it, representing the plight of England!

As she went I felt hushed and solemn, it was an impressive moment; a slight chuckle came from imperturbable Weissman; he had seen too many go to think much of it, and he gave an order for the helm to be put over, so that we might approach the whaler.

They were horribly overcrowded, and were engaged in trying to sort themselves into some sort of order. We passed by them at 50 yards and Weissman, seizing his megaphone, shouted in English: "Goodbye! steer west for America!" A cold horror gripped my heart. It was an awful moment. I dare not write the thoughts that entered my head.

I turned away my head and faced aft, that he should not see my face; looking back I saw the whaler rocking dangerously in our wash, and then a commotion took place in her stern, from which a huge bearded man arose and, shaking his fist in our direction, shouted something or other before his companions pulled him down.

Von Weissman heard and his lips narrowed in. I held my breath in suspense, but he evidently decided against what he had been about to do, for with the order, "Course north! ten knots," he went below.

I remained on deck watching the rapidly receding whaler through my glasses until she was a mere speck—alone on the ocean, 150 miles from land, Then the navigator came up, and with strangely mixed feelings of exultant joy and depressing sorrow I went below.

Von Weissman was in the wardroom. I watched him unobserved. He was humming a tune to himself and had just completed putting a green dot on the chart. This done he lay back on the settee and closed his eyes—strange, insoluble man!

For long hours I could not forget that whaler; I see it now as I write. I suppose I shall get used to it all. What would Zoe say?

The most wonderful thing about man is that he can stand the strain of his own invention of modern war!

* * * * *

I am rather tired to-night, but must just jot down briefly what has taken place to-day, as there is never any time in the daylight hours.

Soon after dawn, at about 8 a.m., we sighted a fair-sized steamer of about 3,000 tons, which we sunk, but I cannot say what she looked like, or whether anyone escaped, as we never came to the surface at all, Von Weissman sighting smoke on the western horizon just as he hit her. We accordingly steered in that direction. However, I think she went almost at once as Von Weissman put a dot (black) on the chart as we made towards number 3.

I very much wanted to know whether there were any survivors, but I did not like to ask him at the time and he has been in such an infernal temper ever since that I haven't had a suitable opportunity.

The cause of his rage was as follows:

Steamer number 3 turned out to be a fine fat chap (of the Clan Line, Von Weissman said, when we first sighted her). We moved in to attack and fired our port bow tube. I waited in vain by the tubes for the expected explosion—nothing happened, but after a couple of minutes a snarl came down the voice pipe: "Surface, GUN ACTION STATIONS!"

I ran aft, and found the Captain white with rage.

"Missed ahead!" he said, with intense feeling, "I'll have to use that confounded gun."

In about three minutes the Captain and myself were on the bridge and the crew were at their stations round the gun.

For the first time I saw the ship; she was stern on and apparently painted with black and white stripes. As I examined her through glasses—she was distant about 3,000 yards—I saw a flash aboard her and a few seconds later a projectile moaned overhead and fell about 6,000 yards over. So she is armed, thought I, and she has actually opened fire on us first.

The effect of this unexpected retort on the part of the Englishman was to throw Weissman into a paroxysm of rage.

"Why don't you fire? What the devil are you waiting for?" etc., etc., were some of the remarks he flung at the gun crew.

I did not consider it advisable to mention to him that they were probably waiting his order to fire, and also his orders for range and deflection, as I had imagined that, here as everywhere else, an officer controls the gun-fire. Apparently in this boat it is not so, as Weissman takes so little interest in his gun that he affects to be, or else actually is, ignorant of the elements of gun control.

At any rate, under the lash of his tongue, the gun's crew soon got into action, the gun-layer taking charge. Our first shot was short, very considerably so, as was also the second. Meanwhile the steamer had been keeping up a very creditably controlled rate of fire, straddling us twice, but missing for deflection, as was natural considering that we were bows on to her.

I felt thoroughly in my element listening to the significant wail of the enemy's shell, punctuated by the ear-splitting report of our own gun. Weissman, gripping the rail with both hands, and to my surprise ducking when one went overhead, watched the target with a fixed expression, but made no attempt to control our gun-fire, which was far from creditable, as is inevitable when it is left to the mercy of the inferior intellect of a seaman.

However, at the tenth or eleventh round we hit her in the upper works, as was shown by a bright red and yellow flash near her funnel. This did not check her firing or speed in the least, in fact she seemed to be gaining on us. She also began to zigzag slightly and throw smoke bombs overboard, which were not so effective from her point of view as I had thought they would be.

Matters were thus for some minutes. We had just hit her aft for the second time, though the shooting was so disgustingly bad that I was about to ask whether I might do the duties of control officer, when there was a blinding flash and the air seemed filled with moaning fragments. When I had recovered from my relief from finding that I was personally uninjured, I observed that two of the gun's crew were wounded and one was lying, either killed or seriously wounded, on the casing. We had been hit in the casing, well forward, and, as was subsequently proved when we dived, little material damage was caused to the boat.

This enemy success caused a temporary cessation of fire. The two wounded men were cautiously making their way aft to the conning tower, and I called for a couple of stokers to come up and carry away the third, when Von Weissman suddenly gave the order to dive. The gun's crew at once made a rush for the conning tower, and were down the hatch in a trice, one of the wounded men fainting at the bottom.

I was unaware as to the reason of this order to dive, and thought that perhaps the Captain had sighted a periscope. As I was turning to precede him down the conning tower hatch I distinctly saw the man lying by the gun lift his hand. I felt I could not leave him there, and instinctively cried, "He is still alive!" But Von Weissman, who was urging the crew to hurry down the hatch, pressed the diving alarm as soon as the last sailor was half in the hatch.

I knew that this meant that the boat would be under in 30 to 40 seconds, so I had no alternative but to get down the hatch as quickly as possible.

I did so with reluctance, and I was followed by Von Weissman, who joined me in the upper conning tower.

I forced myself not to look out of the conning tower scuttles during the few seconds that elapsed as the casing slowly went under, until at last nothing but waving green water showed at each little window. I feared that, if I had looked, I would have seen a wounded man, stung into activity by the cold touch of the Atlantic. Perhaps Von Weissman read my thoughts, or else he remembered my remark concerning the man, for he turned to me and in level tones said:

"Have you any doubt that he was dead?"

I hesitated a moment, and he continued:

"By my direction you have no doubt. He *was*!"

How brutal war is, and what a perfect exponent of the art the Captain proves himself to be! To me a life is a life, a particle of the thing divine; to him a life is a unit, and a half-maimed and probably dying seaman is as nothing in the scales when the safety of a U-boat is at stake. The seamen are numbered in their tens of thousands, the U-boats in their tens. The steamer had hit us once, luckily only in the casing, a second hit might well have punctured the pressure hull, and our fate in these waters would have been certain. Therefore, having summed these things up and balanced them in his mind, he dived and the sailor died.

Once below water Von Weissman seemed more his imperturbable self, and unless I am mistaken he is never really happy on the surface, at least when in action. He is a true water mole.

* * * * *

A day full of interest, though once again I have had to force myself to absorb the horrors of War. I imagine that I am now going through the experiences of a new arrival on the Western Front, who feels a desire to shudder at the sight of every corpse.

At 10 a.m. this morning we sighted the topsails of a sailing boat to the southwest. Closing her on the surface, we approached to within about 6,000 metres, when suddenly Von Weissman ordered "Gun Action Stations."

The gun crew came tumbling up, but not quick enough to suit him, for as they were mustering at the gun he gave the order to dive, only, however, taking her down to periscope depth before instantly ordering surface and then "Gun Action Stations" again. This time we opened fire on the ship, which was a Norwegian barque and, being in the barred zone, liable to destruction.

Von Weissman had announced overnight that at the first opportunity he would give "that—gun's crew a bellyful of practice," and he certainly did. As soon as the first shot was fired, she backed her topsails, and when our fourth shot struck her, somewhere near the foot of the foremast, her crew could be seen hastily abandoning their ship.

This action on their part had no influence with Von Weissman, who had taken personal charge of the helm, and, with the engines running at three-quarter speed, he was zigzagging about, to make it harder for the gun's crew. Every now and then he flung a gibe at the crew, such as suggesting that they should go back to the High Seas Fleet and learn how to shoot.

The sailing ship was soon on fire, for, considering the circumstances, the shooting was very fair, though had I been controlling it I could have confidently guaranteed better results. When she was blazing nicely fore and aft, Von Weissman ordered the practice to cease, and sent the crew below. He then ordered course south, speed ten knots, and I took over the watch.

An hour and a half later, when the navigator gave me a spell, a black cloud on the northern horizon marked the funeral pyre of another of our victims. When I went below, the Captain had just finished playing with his precious old chart.

* * * * *

We received a message at 2 a.m. last night from Heligoland to return forthwith; it is now 2 a.m. and we are approaching the redoubtable Dover Barrage. We had no trouble coming up channel to-day, which seems singularly empty, at any rate in mid-channel, where we were.

* * * * *

We got back about three hours ago, and as I was appointed temporary to the boat, Von Weissman kindly allowed me to leave her and come up to Bruges as soon as we got into the shelters at Zeebrugge.

I got up here just, in time for a late dinner. Hunger satisfied, I retired to my room and, needless to say, at once rang up my darling Zoe.

By the mercy of providence she was in, but imagine my sensations when I heard that that accursed swine of a Colonel was also back from the front, and expected in at the flat at any moment, being then, she thought, engaged in his after dinner drinking bouts at the cavalry officers' club. I could only groan.

A laugh at the other end stung me to furious rage, appeased in an instant by her soothing tones as she told me that I should be glad to hear that he was only up from the Somme on a four-days leave, and was returning next morning by the 8 a.m. troop train. Glad! I could have danced for joy. I breathed again.

As the Colonel was expected back at any moment she thought it advisable to terminate the conversation, which was done with obvious reluctance on her part, or so I flatter myself.

He goes to-morrow, so far so good, but what of the intervening period?

Could any more refined torture be imagined than that I, who love her as I love my own soul, should have to sit here, whilst scarcely a mile away, probably at this very moment as I write, that gross brute is privileged to kiss her, to look at her, to—oh! it's unbearable. When I think of that hog, for though I've never seen him, I've seen his photograph, and I know instinctively that he *is* gross, fresh, as she says, from a drinking bout, should at this moment be permitted to raise his pigs' eyes and look into those glorious wells of violet light; when I think that his is the privilege to see those masses of black hair fall in uncontrolled splendour, then I understand to the full the deep pleasures of murder.

I would give anything to destroy this man, and could shake the Englishman by the hand who fires the delivering bullet!

Steady! Steady! What do I write? No! I mean it, every word of it. Yet of all the mysteries, and to me Zoe is a mass of them, surely the strangest of all is contained in the question: Why does she live with him?

She doesn't love him, she's practically told me so. In fact, I know she doesn't. Let me reason it out by logic. She lives with him, whether voluntarily or involuntarily. Suppose it be voluntarily, then her reasons must be (a) Love; (b) Fascination; (c) Some secret reason. If she is living with him involuntarily it must be: (d) He has a hold on her; (e) For financial reasons.

I strike out at once (a) and (e), for in the case of (e) she knows well that I would provide for her, and (a) I refuse to admit, (b) is hardly credible—I eliminate that. I am left with (c) and (d) which might be the same thing. But what hold can he have on her; she can't have a past, she is too young and sweet for that.

I must find out about this before I go to sea again.

* * * * *

Three days ago, I was racking my brains for the solution of a problem, and, as I see from what I wrote, I was somewhat outside myself. In the interval things have taken an amazing turn. I am still bewildered—but I must put it all down from the beginning.

The Colonel left as she said he would, and I went round to lunch with her.

We had a delightful *tête-à-tête*, and after lunch she played the piano. I was feeling in splendid voice and she accompanied me to perfection in Tchaikowsky's "To the Forest," always a favourite of mine. As the last chords died away, Zoe jumped up from the piano and, with eyes dancing with excitement, placed her hands on my shoulders and exclaimed:

"Karl! I have an idea! I shall make a prisoner of you for two or three days."

I laughed heartily and almost told her that she had already made me a prisoner for life, only I can never get those sort of remarks out quick enough.

But when she said, "No! I am not joking, I mean it," I felt there was more meaning in her sentence than I had at first thought. I begged to be enlightened, and she then unfolded her scheme.

She told me for the first time, that in a forest not far from Bruges she had a little summer-house, to which she used to retreat for week-ends in the hot weather when the Colonel was away. He knew nothing of this country house (she was very insistent on that point), so I imagined she paid for it out of her dress allowance or in some other way. The idea that had just struck her was that she had a sudden fancy to go and spend two days there, and I was to go with her.

I was ready to go to Africa with her if my leave permitted, and it so happened that I was due for four days' overseas leave (limited to Belgian territory) so that this fitted in very well, and I told her so.

She was delighted, then, with one of those quick intuitions which women are so clever at, she read the half-formed thought in my mind, and said: "You mustn't think it's not going to be conventional; old Babette will be with us to chaperon me." Old Babette is an aged female whom she calls her maid. I think she is jealous of me.

I agreed at once that of course I quite understood it was to be highly conventional, etc., though I smiled to myself as I visualized my mother's shocked face and uplifted hands had she heard my Zoe's ideas on the conventions.

I was trying to fathom what was at the bottom of it all when she remarked: "Of course, as my prisoner you will have to obey all my orders."

I replied that this was certainly so.

"And one of the first things," she continued, "that happens to a prisoner when he goes through the enemy lines is that he is blindfolded, and in the same way I shan't let you know where you are going."

Seeing a doubtful look in my eyes as I endeavoured to keep pace with the underlying idea, if any, of this truly feminine fancy, she suddenly came up to me and, lifting her eyes to mine, murmured: "Don't you trust me?"

In a moment my passion flared up, and rained hot kisses on her face as she struggled to release herself from my arms.

When I left that night after dinner, and, walking on air, returned to the Mess, it was arranged that I should be at her flat with my suit-case at 6 p.m. the next evening, prepared, to use her own words, "to disappear with me for 48 hours."

She had told me of an address in Bruges which she said would forward on any telegram if I was recalled, and I had to be satisfied with that, for I may as well say here that I never discovered where I went to, and I don't know to this moment in what part of Belgium I spent the last two nights.

I tried to find out at first, but as she obviously attached some importance to keeping the locality of her woodland retreat a secret, probably to circumvent the Colonel, I soon gave up trying to get the secret from her, and contented myself with taking things as they came.

To go on with my account of what happened—which was really so remarkable that I propose writing it out in detail to the best of my memory—at 6 p.m. next day I was naturally at her flat feeling very much as if I was on the threshold of an adventure.

Zoe was excited and the flat was in a turmoil, as apparently she had only just begun to pack her dressing-case.

Soon after six we went down and got into a large Mercédès car which I had noticed standing outside when I arrived. We were soon on our way, and left Bruges by the Eastern barrier; we showed our passes and proceeded into the darkened country-side. We had been running for about a mile when she remarked, "Prisoners will now be blindfolded!" and, to my astonishment, slipped a little black silk bag over my head.

I was so startled I didn't know whether to be angry, or to laugh, or what to do. Eventually I did nothing, and, entering into the spirit of the game, declared that even a wretched prisoner had the right not to be stifled, whereupon she lifted the lower portion of the bag and uncovered my mouth. Shortly afterwards I was electrified to feel a pair of soft lips meet mine, a sensation which was repeated at frequent intervals, and, as I whispered in her ear, under these conditions I was prepared to be taken prisoner into the jaws of hell.

This pleasant journey had lasted for about three-quarters of an hour when my mask was removed and I was informed that I was "inside the enemy lines!" Through the windows of the car I could dimly see that an apparently endless mass of fir trees were rushing past on each side. This state of affairs continued for a kilometre or so, when we branched to the right and soon entered a large clearing in the forest, at one side of which stood the house. Babette, Zoe and myself entered the building, and the car disappeared, presumably back to Bruges.

The house, built of logs, was of two stories; on the ground floor were two living rooms, and the domains of Babette, who amongst her other accomplishments turned out to be not only a most capable valet, but a first-class cook. On the second story there were two large rooms. The whole house was furnished after the manner of a hunting lodge, with stags' heads on the walls, and skins on the floors. In the drawing-room there was a piano and a few etchings of the wild boar by Schaffein.

I dressed for dinner in my "smoking," though under ordinary circumstances I should have considered this rather formal, but I was glad I did, for she appeared in full evening *tenue*. She wore a violet gown, and across her forehead a black satin bandeau with a Z in diamonds upon it. It must have cost two thousand marks, and I wondered with a dull kind of jealousy whether the Colonel had given it to her.

I cannot remember of what we talked during dinner. We have a hundred subjects in common, and we look at so many aspects of the world through the same pair of eyes; I only know that when I have been talking to her for a period—there is no exact measurement of time for me when I am with her—I leave her presence feeling "completed." I feel that a sort of gap within my being has been filled, that a spiritual hunger has been satisfied, that I have got something which I wanted, but for which I could not have formulated the desire in words. I had resolved that on this first night I would bring matters between us to a head and end this delicious but intolerable uncertainty as to how we stood; yet, when old Babette had served us with coffee in the drawing-room, as I call the second living-room, and we were alone together, I could not bring up the subject. Partly because I think she prevented me so doing by that skilful shepherding of the conversation into other paths with an artfulness with which God endows all women, and also partly because I could not screw myself up to the pitch. I could not, or rather would not, put my fate to the touch. I had a presentiment that in reaching for the summit I might fall from the slope. Alas! how true was this foreboding in some senses—but I will keep all things in their right order.

"The track met our ram."

In the flash I caught a glimpse of his conning tower

Let it only be recorded that when she kissed me good-night (with the tenderness of a mother) and left me to smoke a final cigar I had said nothing, and I could only wonder at the strange fate that had placed me practically alone with a girl whom I had grown to love with a deep emotion, and who appeared to love me, yet often behaved as if I was her brother.

The next day we were like two children. The snow was deep on the ground, and the fir trees stood like thousands of sentinels in grey uniform round the clearing. Once during the afternoon, as with Zoe's assistance I was furiously chopping wood for the fire, a droning noise made me look up, and thousands of metres overhead a small squadron of aeroplanes, evidently bound for the Western Front, sailed slowly across the sky. I thought how awkward it would be for them if they experienced an engine failure whilst over the forest, though they were up so high that I imagine they could have glided ten kilometres, and as I think (but I am not certain, and I have pledged myself not to try and find out) we were in the Forest of Montellan, which is barely fifteen kilometres broad, I suppose they could have fallen clear of the trees.

As a matter of fact I imagine they would have used our clearing—I'm glad they didn't.

That night after dinner she played to me, first Beethoven and then Chopin. I can see her as I write; she had just finished the 14th Prelude and, resting her chin on her hand, she smiled mysteriously at me.

The hour had come, and, driven by strong impulses, I spoke. I told her that I loved her as I had never thought that a man could love a woman; I told her that I longed to shield her and protect her, and above all things to remove her from the clutches of that bestial Colonel, and as I bent over her and felt my senses swim in the subtleties of her perfume, I begged her passionately to say the word that would give me the right to fight the world on her behalf.

When I had finished she was silent for a long while, and I can remember distinctly that I wondered whether she could hear the thump! thump!

thump! of my heart, which to my agitated mind seemed to beat with the strength of a hammer.

At length she spoke; two words came slowly from her lips:

"I cannot."

I was not discouraged. I could see, I could feel, that a tremendous struggle was raging, the outward signs of which were concealed by her averted head.

At length I asked her point-blank whether she loved me. Her silence gave me my answer, and I took her unresisting body into my arms and kissed her to distraction. Oh! these kisses, how bitter they seem to me now, and yet how I long to hold her once again. For, freeing herself from my embrace and speaking almost mechanically, she said:

"Karl! I must tell you. I cannot marry you."

I pleaded, I prayed, I argued, I demanded. It was in vain; I always came up against the immovable "I cannot."

And then I crashed over the precipice towards whose edge I had been blindly going. I had said for the hundredth time, "But you know you love me," when with a sob she abandoned all reserve, and, flinging her arms round my neck, implored me to take her. Then, as I caught my breath, she quickly said, as if frightened that she had gone too far, "But I cannot marry you."

I looked down into those beautiful eyes, and for the first time I understood. For perhaps ten seconds I battled for my soul and the purity of our love; then, tearing my sight from those eyes which would lure an archangel to destruction, I was once more master of my body. As my resolution grew, I hated her for doing this thing that had wrecked in an instant the hopes of months, the ideals on which I had begun to build afresh my life.

She felt the change, and left me.

As she went out by the door she gave me one last look, a look in which love struggled with shame, a look which no man has ever earned the right to receive from any woman.

But I was as a statue of marble, dazed by this calamity.

As the door closed upon her, I started forward—it was too late.

Had she waited another instant—but there, I write of what has happened and not what might have been.

I did not sleep that night, until the dawn began to separate each fir tree from the black mass of the forest. Twice in the night, with shame I confess it, I opened my door and looked down the little passage-way; and twice I closed the door and threw myself upon my bed in an agony of torment. It was ten o'clock when a knock at the door aroused me, and the sunlight through the window-pane was tracing patterns on the floor.

There was a note on the breakfast table, but before I opened it I knew that, save for Babette, I was alone in the house.

The note was brief, unaddressed and unsigned. I have it here before me; I have meant to tear it up but I cannot. It is a weakness to keep it, but I have lost so much in the last few days, that I will not grudge myself some small relic of what has been. The note says:

"I am leaving for Bruges at half-past eight, when the car was ordered to fetch us back. I go alone. Babette will give you breakfast. The car will return for you at eleven o'clock. I rely on your honour in that you will not observe where you have been. Come to me when you want me—till then, farewell."

It was as she said, and I honourably acceded to her request. This afternoon just before lunch I arrived in Bruges, and since tea-time I have tried to write down what has happened since I left the day before yesterday. Oh! how could she do it, how can it be possible that she is a woman like that? I could have sworn that she was not like this—and yet how can I account for her life with the Colonel? There must be some reason, but in Heaven's name, what?

Meanwhile I am to go to her when I want her! And that will be when I can give her my name. But oh! Zoe, I want you now, so badly, oh! so badly!

* * * * *

I saw her once to-day in the gardens, walking by herself.

* * * * *

I have told Max's secretary that I want to get to sea; to be here in Bruges and not to see her is more than I can bear.

I sail at dawn to-morrow. Shall I see her? No, it is best not.

A frightful noise over the New Year celebrations to-night. Champagne flowing like water in the Mess. I feel the year 1917 opens badly for me.

Weissman also went to sea again for a short trip in the Channel, and has not reported for five days. Perhaps he has despised the Dover Barrage once too often. If this is so, it is a great loss to the service: he was a man of iron resolution in underwater attack.

I feel I ought to despise Zoe, but I can't. I love her too much; after all, am I not perhaps encasing myself in the robe of a Pharisee?

She offered me all she had, save only the one thing I asked, without which I will take nothing. I cannot reconcile her behaviour with her character; why can't she trust me? why can't she be frank with me? I will not believe she is that sort.

I feel I cannot go out again without a *sign*—I may not return, and I will not leave her, perhaps for ever, with this bitterness between us.

* * * * *

At sea in U.C.47 again. Alten as surly as ever.

I decided finally to write to Zoe, but found it difficult to know what to say. Eventually I said more than I had intended. I told her frankly that I experienced a shock, but that I had not meant to seem so cold, and that what I had done had been done for both our sakes. I told her that I still loved her, and I implored her once more to leave the Colonel and come to me as my wife.

Already I long to know what message awaits me on my return.

This will not be for three days. We left at dawn this morning to lay mines off the channel to Harwich harbour; a nest from which submarines, cruisers and destroyers buzz in and out like wasps. It will be ticklish work.

On the bottom.

Our mines are still with us, but so are our lives, which is something.

We were approaching the appointed spot at 6 a.m. this morning, when without the slightest warning the track of a torpedo was seen streaking towards us about 50 yards on the starboard bow.

Before Alten (who was on the bridge with me) could do more than press the diving alarm, the track met our ram. I breathed again, and was then reminded by an oath from Alten that the boat was diving.

It was evident that we had only been saved by the torpedo running deep under the cut-away part of our bow, otherwise!—well, the tangle of my affairs would have been easily straightened.

Further procedure on the surface was suicidal, and we kept hydrophone patrol, twice hearing the motors of the enemy submarine. At the moment we are on the bottom waiting to come up and charge to-night, and lay our mines at dawn to-morrow.

* * * * *

On the bottom in 28 metres and feeling none too comfortable, as there would appear to be about a dozen destroyers overhead.

Last night, or rather early this morning, I participated in one of the most extraordinary incidents that I have ever heard of.

It was pitch-black dark when I took over at 4 a.m., and a fresh breeze had raised a lumpy sea, which covered the bridge with spray. We were charging 400 amps on each, with the intention of laying one mine directly there was sufficient light to get a fix from some of the buoys which the

English stick down all over the place here in the most convenient manner possible. If only one could believe they never shifted them. Alten says it never occurs to an Englishman to do a thing like that, but I'm not so sure. However, we were proceeding along at about five knots, crashing into the sea rather badly, when out of the black beastliness of the night I saw a shape close aboard on the port hand.

As I hesitated for a second as to my course of action, I was astounded to see a large submarine which must have been British, on an opposite course, not more than 25 metres away!

This sounds absurd, but it really wasn't further. I'm not ashamed to confess that I was completely disorganized; it did not seem possible that the enemy was literally alongside me.

I don't know how it struck the officer in the British boat, but I must give him credit for doing something first, for he fired a Very's white light straight at me as the two boats passed. It impinged on the hull, and in the flash I caught a photographic glimpse of his conning tower, on which was painted the letter E, followed by two numbers, of which one was a two I think, and the other a nine.

By this time he was on my port quarter and rapidly disappearing; in a frenzy of rage I managed to get my revolver out, and whilst with the left hand I pressed the diving alarm, with the right hand I emptied the magazine in his direction. When we were down, Alten practically refused to believe me, which made me very pleased that in descending I had trod on a pair of hands which turned out to be his, as he had started up the ladder to the upper conning tower when he first heard the alarm.

I presume our opponent dived as well, but evidently he had put two and two together and used his aerial at some period, for when at dawn we poked a periscope up, a flotilla of destroyers appeared to be looking for something, which "something" was us, unless I am much mistaken; so we bottomed, where we have been ever since. The Hydroplane Operator keeps up a monotonous sing-song to the effect that "Fast running propellers are either receding or approaching." The crew are collected round the mine-tubes as I write, and are singing a lugubrious song, the refrain of which runs:

> "Death for the Fatherland! Glorious fate,
> This is the end that we gladly await."

Why will the seamen always become morbid when possible? And there is not a man amongst them who is not inwardly thinking of some beer-hall in Bruges, though I suppose that like their betters they have their romances of a tenderer kind.

* * * * *

The boat has been rolling about on the bottom in the most sickening manner the whole afternoon. We flooded P and Q to capacity, which gave her 50 tons negative, but it seems to have little effect in steadying her, and it is evident that a really heavy gale is running on top.

* * * * *

Surfaced at 10 p.m.; a very heavy sea running and impossible to do much more than heave to. This weather has one point in its favour and that is that the destroyers are driven in.

It got steadily worse all night, and at midnight we lost our foremost wireless mast overboard; we have now (10 a.m.) been 48 hours without communication. At dawn we could see nothing to fix by; not a buoy in sight, nothing but an expanse of foam-topped short steep waves of dirty neutral-tinted water; how different to the great green and white surges of the broad Atlantic.

Under these circumstances Alten decided to risk it and return without laying our mines; for once in a way I agreed with him, as it is better not to lay a minefield at all than dump one down in some unknown position which one may have to traverse oneself in the course of a month or so. We are now slowly, very slowly, struggling back to Zeebrugge.

A green sea came down the conning tower to-day, and everything in the boat is damp and smelly and beastly. The propellers race at frequent intervals and the whole boat shudders—I feel miserable.

Alten has started to drink spirits; he began as soon as we decided to go back. He will be incapable by to-night, and it means that I shall have to take her in.

What hell this is, sitting in sodden clothes, with the stench of four days' living assaulting the nostrils, and a motion of the devil; the glass is very low and is slowly rising, so that I suppose it will blow harder soon, though it is about force eight at present.

I wonder what Zoe will have written in reply to my note. When I think of what I rejected and compare it with my beast-like existence here, I can hardly believe that I behaved as I did—what would I not give now to be transported back to the forest! At this rate of progress we shall take another 24 hours. I wonder if I can knock another half-knot out of her without smashing her up.

* * * * *

The extraordinarily violent motion has upset the *Anschutz*.[14] The bearing cone of the stabilizing gyro has cracked, and the master compass began to wander off in circles. I was just resting for an hour or two, wedged up on a wet settee with coats equally wet, when her heavy pitching changed to a wallowing roll, and I heard the pilot, who was on watch, cursing down the voice-pipe, as we had sagged off our course.

I heard the voice of the helmsman querulously maintain that he was steering his course by *Anschutz*, so I got up and gingerly clawed my way into the control room, where I found by comparing *Anschutz* with

---

14 Gyroscopic compass.—ETIENNE.

magnetic that the former had gone to hell, the reason being obvious, as the stabilizer was exerting a strongly biased torque. I stopped the *Anschutz* and asked the pilot to give the helmsman a steady by magnetic.

As we staggered back to our course I heard a thud in the wardroom, and on returning to my settee found that Alten had rolled out of his bunk, where he was lying in a drunken stupor, and that he was face downwards, sprawling on the deck, half his face in the broken half of a dirty dish which had fallen off the table whilst I was having tea. As I couldn't let the crew see him like this, I was obliged to struggle and get him back into his bunk. He was like a log and absolutely incapable of rendering me any assistance, though he did open his eyes and mutter once or twice as I lifted him up, trunk first and then his legs. He stank of spirits and I hated touching him. Lord! what a truly hoggish man he is; yet I cannot help envying him his oblivion to these surroundings.

* * * * *

Arrived in, this afternoon.

Alten quite slept off his drink, and was offensively sarcastic as I worked on the forepart with wires, getting her into the shelters alongside the mole.

I hastened up to Bruges, and in the Mess heard several items of news and found two letters. The first, in a well-known handwriting, I opened eagerly, but received a chill of disappointment when I read its single line.

"I am here when you want me.—Z."

So she thinks to break my resolution!

No! I am stronger than she, and, now that I know she loves me, I can and will bend her to my will. Even now, at this distance of time, I can hardly understand my conduct the other day. I must have been given the strength of ten. I feel that I could not do it again; had she hesitated a second longer at the door—well, I can hardly say what I would have done.

It is my duty to do so, for her sake and my own. But I know my weakness, and in this fact lies my strength. Cost what it may, I shall not permit myself to go near her until she yields.

The second letter gave me a great surprise. It was from Rosa. She has passed some examination, and is coming *here* of all places as a Red Cross nurse. She says she is looking forward to going round a U-boat! She assumes a good deal, I must say, still, I suppose I must be polite to her; but why the deuce does she sign herself "Yours, Rosa?" She's not mine, and I don't want her; it seems funny to me that I once thought of her vaguely in that sort of way. Now, I feel rather disturbed that she is coming here, though I don't quite see why I should worry, and yet I wonder if it is a coincidence her coming to Bruges?

I'm almost inclined to think it isn't. After all, every girl wants to get married, and without conceit my family, circumstances and, in the privacy of the pages of this journal I may add, my personal appearances, are such as would appeal to most girls—except Zoe, apparently!

I'll have to be on my guard against Miss Rosa.

I heard to-day that I am likely to be appointed to the periscope school in a few weeks' time, and meanwhile I am to be attached as supernumerary to the operations division on old Max's staff.

* * * * *

The work here is most interesting. I feel glad that I am one of the spiders weaving the web for Britain's destruction.

The impasse with Zoe still continues, and my peace of mind has been still further disturbed by the actual arrival of Rosa. She rang me up within twelve hours of her arrival, and, of course, I was obliged to call. That was the day before yesterday. Rosa is at the No. 3 Hospital here, and was horribly effusive. Some people would, I suppose, call her good-looking, but to me, with my mind's-eye in perpetual contemplation of my darling Zoe, Rosa looked like a turnip. Her first movement after the preliminary greetings was to offer me a cigarette! I then noticed that her fingers were stained with nicotine, unpleasant in a man, disgusting in a woman.

Her nose was shiny and greasy—horrible. After a little talk she volunteered the statement that yesterday was her afternoon off, and she was simply longing to have tea in the gardens.

I endeavoured to make some feeble excuse on the grounds of the weather being unsuitable, but I am no good at these social lies, and I was eventually obliged to promise to take her there. I was the more annoyed in that her main object was obviously to be seen walking with a U-boat officer.

Accordingly, yesterday, I found myself walking about with her at my side. My feelings can better be imagined than described when I suddenly saw Zoe, accompanied by Babette, in the distance. I hastily altered course, and pray she didn't see me.

In the course of the afternoon Rosa had the impertinence to say that at Frankfurt they were saying that I was interested in a beautiful widow at Bruges, and could she (Rosa) write and say I was heart-whole, or else what the girl was like. I'm afraid that I lost my temper a little, and I told Rosa she could write to all the busybodies at home and tell them from me to go to the devil.

These women in the home circle, and especially aunts, are always the same; firstly, they badger one to get married, and then if they think one is contemplating such a step they are all agog to find out whether she is suitable!

* * * * *

Three more boats, two of which are U.C.'s, are overdue. It is distinctly unpleasant not knowing how or where they go, though the U.B. boat (Friederich Althofen) made her incoming position the day before yesterday as off Dungeness, so it looks as if the barrage at Dover which got Weissman has got Althofen as well. I wonder what new devilry they have put down there.

How one wishes that in 1914, instead of seeking the capture of Paris, we had realized the importance of the Channel Ports to England, and struck for them!

It would not have been necessary to strike even in September, 1914. We could have walked into them. Dunkirk, at all events, should have been ours; however, we must do the best with things as they are, not that I would consider it too late even now to make a big push for the French coast.

It would seem, as a matter of fact, that all the pushing is to be at the other end of the line, in the Verdun sector, from the rumours I hear, though I should have thought once bitten twice shy in that quarter.

* * * * *

Saw Zoe again in the distance, and I think she saw me; at all events she turned round and walked away.

This girl whom I cannot, and would not if I could, obliterate from my thoughts, is causing me much worry.

She shows no sign of giving in, and I for one intend to be adamant. I shall defeat her in time. The male intellect is always ultimately victorious, other things being equal. I was reading Schopenhauer on the subject last night. What a brain that man had, though I confess his analysis of the female mentality is so terribly and truthfully cruel that it jars on certain of my feelings.

Zoe's resolution in this conflict, this sex war one might call it, only adds to her charm in my eyes; she is, I feel, a worthy mate for me, both intellectually and physically, and she shall be mine—I have decided it.

Met Rosa to-day at old Max's house, where I went to pay a duty call.

Her Excellency is as forbidding a specimen of her sex as any I have ever met. She quite frightened me, and in the home circle the old man seemed quite subdued.

I escorted Rosa home, and on the way to her hospital she gave me a great surprise, as after much evasive talk she suddenly came out with the news that she was engaged to Heinrich Baumer, of U.C.23. I was quite taken aback, and will frankly confess that not so very long ago I imagined, evidently erroneously, that she was disposed to let her affections become engaged in another quarter. However, I was really very glad to hear this news, and congratulated her with genuine feeling.

The knowledge that she was a promised woman quite altered my feelings towards her, and before I quite meant to, I had told her a considerable amount about Zoe. It gave me much relief to be able to unburden myself, and confide my difficulties elsewhere than in the pages of this journal.

I have asked the girl to tea to-morrow.

* * * * *

A vile air raid last night. British machines, of course. They seemed determined to get over the town, and from 1 a.m. to 3 a.m. relays of machines (of which not *one* was shot down) attacked us. The din was tremendous, and all sleep was out of the question.

Morning revealed surprisingly little damage, as is often the case in these big raids, whereas a few bombs from a chance machine often work havoc. I was down at 50 B.C. aerodrome this morning, and heard that as soon as the moon suits we are going to make Dunkirk sit up as retaliation for last night's efforts. There were also rumours of big attacks impending on London as soon as the new type of Gothas are delivered. That will shake the smug security of those cursed islanders.

Rosa came to tea, and afterwards I told her more about Zoe, and as I expect any day to be appointed to the periscope school at Kiel, I asked Rosa to try and effect an introduction to Zoe, and do what she could for me. Rosa gave me the impression that she was somewhat surprised that I should have had any difficulty with Zoe (of course I had not told her of the shooting-box scene). Rosa evidently thinks any woman ought to be honoured . . .

Perhaps I was not so far wrong in my surmises as to Rosa's previous inclinations—I wonder; at any rate she will undoubtedly make Baumer a good wife, and she will probably be very fruitful and grow still fatter and housewifely. She is of a type of woman appointed by God in his foresight as breeders. Zoe, my adorable one, will probably not take kindly to babies.

* * * * *

I am ordered to report myself at Kiel by next Monday.

I am terribly tempted to ring up Zoe on the telephone before I leave: it seems dreadful to leave her without a word; but at the same time I feel that she would interpret this as a sign of weakness on my part—as indeed it would be. I must be firm, for strength of mind pays with women, even more than with men.

At Kiel.

I left Bruges without a word either to or from my obstinate darling.

It is torture being away from her. I had thought that when I was here and not exposed to the temptation of going round and seeing her, that it would be easier; it is not. I long to write, and how I wonder whether she is feeling it as I do.

I have read somewhere that a woman's passion once aroused is more ungovernable than a man's. That her whole being cries aloud for me cannot be doubted, and if the above statement is true what inflexibility of will she must be showing—it almost makes me fear—but no, I will defeat her in this strange contest, and she shall be my wife.

The work here is strenuous, and the grass does not grow under one's feet. The course for commanding officers lasts four weeks, and terminates in an exceedingly practical but rather fearsome test—i.e., they have six steamers here camouflaged after the English fashion with dazzle painting, and these six steamers, protected by launches and harbour defence craft, steam across Kiel Bay in the manner of a convoy. The officer being examined has to attack this group of ships in one of the instructional submarines, and in three attacks he must score at least two hits, or else, in theory, he is returned to general service in the Fleet.

Fortunately at the moment I hear that owing to recent losses they are distinctly on the short side where submarine officers are concerned, so they'll probably make it easy when I do my test.

* * * * *

I see I have written nothing here for a fortnight; this is due to two causes: Firstly, I have been so extraordinarily busy, and, secondly, I have been most depressed through a letter I received from Fritz. It contained two items of bad news.

In the first place, I heard for the first time of the tragedy of Heinrich Baumer's boat, and to my astonishment Fritz tells me that Rosa and another girl were in her when she was lost!

It appears that she was to go out for a couple of hours' diving off the port as a matter of routine after her two months' overhaul. She went out at 10 a.m., and was sighted from the signal station at the end of the mole at 11.30, when almost immediately afterwards there was an explosion and she disappeared. Motor-boats were quickly on the scene, but only debris came to the surface. Divers were sent down, and reported that she was in ten metres of water completely shattered. It is assumed, for lack of other explanation, that she struck a chance drifting mine which was moving down the coast on the tide.

Meanwhile Rosa and another sister were missing from the hospital, and after forty-eight hours someone put two and two together and started investigations. It has been ascertained that Baumer motored down from Bruges after breakfast, and that in the car were two figures taken to be sailors, as they were muffled up in oilskins. This fact was noted by the control sentries, as, though the day was showery, it was not raining hard. Other scraps of evidence unite in showing that these were the two girls who had apparently induced Baumer to take them out for a dive as a treat.

What a tragedy! However, it must have been quite instantaneous. Poor Rosa, with all her vanities about war work, to think that the war would claim her like that![15]

Fritz added that old Max is almost off his head with rage over the whole business, and it is difficult to say whether he is more angry over Baumer and the boat being lost, or over the fact that Baumer being dead he is unable to administer those "disciplinary actions" in which he delights.

* * * * *

Great excitement here, as the day after to-morrow His Imperial Majesty the Kaiser and Hindenburg are due to pay Kiel a surprise visit. We are to be inspected and addressed. Tremendous preparations are going on.

* * * * *

---

[15] It is known that a boat with women on board was lost whilst exercising off Zeebrugge in the Spring of 1917. This would appear to be the boat in question.—ETIENNE.

His Majesty, accompanied by the great Field-Marshal, inspected us this morning, and made a fine speech, of which we have been given printed copies. I shall frame mine and hang it in my boat, if I get a command.

I transcribe it:

"Officers and men of the U-boat service:

"In the midst of the anxious moments in which we live I have determined to make time to come and witness in my own person the labours of those on whom I and the Fatherland rely. Fresh from the great battles on the West which are gnawing at the vitals of our hereditary enemies, I come to those whose glorious mission it will be to strike relentlessly at our most deadly and cunning enemy—cursed Britain. God is on our side and will protect you at sea for, in the striking at the nation which openly boasts that it aims at starving our women and children, you are engaged on a mission of undoubted holiness.

"You must sink and destroy even as of old the Israelites smote and destroyed the alien races.

"To the officers I would particularly say, my person is your honour, and I am your supreme chief. From my hands you will receive honour, and from my hands will proceed just punishment for the unhappy ones who fail in their duty.

"To the men I would say, trust and obey your officers as you would your God. Officers and men! In you, your Kaiser and Fatherland place their trust—let neither be disappointed!"

After his address, His Majesty graciously spoke a few words to individuals, of whom I had the signal honour of being one. I felt that I was in the presence of an Emperor. His gestures, his eyes, his voice, impressed me as belonging to a man born to command and to fill high places. The Field-Marshal never opened his mouth. I understand from his A.D.C. that he rarely speaks in public.

* * * * *

The Colonel is KILLED! When I think about it, I am so excited I can hardly write!

I heard the great news last night, quite by accident. I was sitting in the Mess after dinner, and picked up *Die Woche*, and glancing at the pictures, I suddenly saw the portrait of Colonel Stein, of the Brandenburgers, killed on the 7th instant near Ypres. I recognized the ugly and bloated face immediately from the photograph of him which she had once shown me.

My first impulse was to send her a wire, but, on thinking matters over, I decided that it would be difficult to put all my thoughts into the curt sentences of a telegram, and, further, that as all wires are doubtless examined at the Main Post Office at Bruges, it might lead to trouble, so I wrote her a letter.

This, in a way, has been an exhibition of weakness on my part, as I had promised myself that I would not take the first step in reopening communication; but I feel that the fortunate death of Stein has completely altered the case. I told her in the letter that I realized that I had made mistakes, but that if she still loved me with half the strength that I loved her, then a telegram to me would make me the happiest of men.

I wrote that yesterday, but have had no wire. Perhaps, like me, she distrusts telegrams and prefers letters.

* * * * *

A long letter from Zoe: an accursed fetter—an abominable letter—a damnable letter; she still refuses to marry me. I leave for Bruges to-night on forty-eight hours' special leave.

Kiel, 17th.

I hate Zoe, she has broken my heart.

After her preposterous letter of the 14th, I decided that in a matter which so closely affected my happiness no stone ought to remain unturned to ensure a satisfactory solution of the problem, so I determined to have a personal interview. I arrived at Bruges after tea and went at once to the flat.

I tackled her immediately on the subject of her letter, and told her that naturally I understood that a decent interval must elapse before we married; but, granted this fact, I told her that I failed to see what prevented our marriage.

A most unpleasant and harrowing scene ensued, the details of which form such painful recollections that I really cannot write them down here, though in the passage of months I have acquired the habit of writing in the pages of this journal with the same freedom as I would talk to that wife whom I had hoped to possess. She maintained an obstinate silence when I urged her to give me at least some tangible reason as to why she would not marry me. She contented herself and maddened me by reflecting in a kind of monotone: "I love you, Karl! and am yours, but I cannot marry you."

I could have beaten her till she was senseless, but I had enough sense to realize that with Zoe, whose resolution, considering she is a woman, amazes me, force is not the best method. As I continued to press her (time was important: had I not journeyed far to see her?), those glorious eyes of hers, which I love and whose power I dread, filled with tears. I was a brute! I was heartless! I was inconsiderate! I could not love her! I was cruel! And I know not what other accusation crushed me down.

Broken-hearted and dispirited, I told her to choose there and then.

She collapsed on to a sofa in a storm of tears, and after a severe mental struggle I took the only possible course, and leaving the room—left her for ever. I have resumed my service life determined to cast her out from my mind.

I will not deceive myself: it will be hard. Love and Logic are deadly enemies, but Logic must and shall prevail. Though I have seen her for the last time, I cannot escape the net of fascination which the girl has thrown over me. Perhaps in the course of time I shall slowly emerge and free myself from its entanglements. At present I hate her for this blow she has dealt me, and yet, O Zoe! my darling, how I long to be with you!

* * * * *

To-day I went through my final test for qualification as U-boat commander.

At 9 a.m. I proceeded to sea in command of the U.11, one of the instructional boats here. We proceeded out into Kiel Bay. On board and watching my every movement was a committee consisting of a commander and two lieutenant-commanders.

On arrival at the entrance lightship, I was ordered to attack a convoy of camouflaged ships which were just visible about fifteen kilometres away off the Spit Bank. I had a very shrewd idea as to the course they would steer, and on coming up for my final observation I found myself in an excellent position, 1,000 metres on the bow of the leading ship. The rest was easy. I gave the leader the two bow torpedoes, and, turning sixteen points, fired my stern tube at the third ship of the line. Two hits were obtained, and I returned to harbour well pleased with myself. There is not the slightest chance of having failed to qualify.

* * * * *

My confidence in myself was not misplaced; I heard to-day that I am on the command list, and anticipate in a few days being appointed to a boat. I wonder which craft I shall get?

* * * * *

I met the A.D.C. to the Chief of the Staff at the school, at the gardens, and in conversation with him discovered that he had heard that three boats were being detached from the Flanders flotilla for an unknown destination. This has given me an idea, for I feel that I can never return to Bruges, and I was rather dreading being appointed to one of the boats there. I have dropped a line to Fritz Regels, who is on old Max's staff, and told him that I do not wish to return to Bruges, and I further hinted that I understood a detached squadron was proceeding somewhere, and, as far as I was concerned, the further the better, if I could get into it.

I have tried the night life at this place at the Mascotte and Trocadero,[16] in order to forget, but it is a poor consolation.

* * * * *

A letter from Fritz, saying that he has an idea that Korting's boat would suit me, though he could not of course give me further details in a letter; however, he informs me positively that I shall not be at Bruges.

On the strength of this I have wired to Fritz, and asked him to try and fix up an exchange between me and Korting, provided the latter is agreeable and the people in Max's office have no objection. I have a recollection that Korting's boat is one of the U.40—U.60 class, which would suit me admirably, and, as for destination, I care not where it is, provided only that it be far from Bruges.

At sea.

I have quite neglected my poor old journal for several weeks. But I have passed through an extraordinarily busy period.

It was approved that I should relieve Korting, whose boat, the U.59, I discovered to be refitting at Wilhelmshaven. I was very pleased not to go back to Bruges, though as we steam steadily north at this moment I cannot escape a sense of deep disappointment that upon my return from this trip I shall not enjoy as of old the fascination of Zoe. But I shall have plenty of time to get accustomed to this idea, for this is no ordinary trip.

---

16 Two well-known cabarets at Kiel.—ETIENNE.

We are bound for the North Cape and Murman Coast, where we remain until well into the cold weather—at any rate, for three months.

Our mission is to work off that fogbound and desolate coast, and attack the constant stream of traffic between England and Archangel. There are two other boats besides ourselves on the job, but we shall all be working far apart.

Our first billet is off the North Cape. In order to save time, we are to be provisioned once a month in one of the fjords. I don't imagine the Admiralty will have any difficulty in getting supplies up to us, as at the moment we are off the Lofotens, and we actually have not had to dive since we left the Bight!

There seems to be nothing on the sea except ourselves. Where is the much vaunted and impenetrable web of blockade which the English are supposed to have spread around us? And yet many raw materials are getting very short with us. I see that in this boat they have replaced several copper pipes with steel ones during her refit, and this will lead to trouble unless we are careful—steel pipes corrode so badly that I never feel ready to trust them for pressure work.

The truth about the blockade is that it is largely a paper blockade, yet not ineffective for all that. Unfortunately for us, the damned English and their hangers-on control the cables of the world, and hence all the markets, and I don't suppose, to take the case of copper, that a single pound of it is mined from the Rio Tinto without the British Board of Trade knowing all about it. The neutral firms simply dare not risk getting put on to the British Black List; it means ruination for them. And then all these dollar-grabbing Yankees, enjoying all the advantages of war without any of its dangers—they make me sick.

This seems a most profitable job. I have only been up seven days, but I've bagged four steamers, all by gun-fire, and all fat ships, brimful of stuff for the Russians. My practice has been to make the North Cape every day or two to fix position, as the currents are the most abnormal in these parts, and I should say that the "Sailing Directions Pilotage

Handbook" and "Tidal Charts" were compiled by a gentleman at a desk who had never visited these latitudes.

At the moment I am standing well out to sea, as the immediate vicinity of the North Cape has become rather unhealthy.

Yesterday afternoon (I had sunk number four in the morning, and the crew were still pulling for the coast) four British trawlers turned up. These damned little craft seem to turn up wherever one goes. I longed to have a bang at them with my gun, but, apart from the uncertainty as to what they carried in the way of armament, I have strict orders to avoid all that sort of thing, so I dived and steamed slowly west, came up at dusk and proceeded to charge up my batteries.

These U.60's are excellent boats, and I am very lucky to get one so soon. I suppose Korting, being a married man, wants to stay near his wife. I cannot write that word without painful memories of Zoe and idle thoughts of what might have been. Well, perhaps it is for the best. I am not sure that a member of the U-boat service has the right to get married in war-time, for unless he is of exceptional mentality it must affect his outlook under certain circumstances, though I think I should have been an exception here. Then the anxiety to the woman must be enormous; as every trip comes round a voice must cry within her, this may be the last. The contrast between the times in harbour and the trips is so violent, so shattering and clear cut.

With a soldier's wife, she merely knows that he is at the front; with us, at 8 p.m. one may be kissing one's wife in Bruges, and at 6 a.m. creeping with nerves on edge through the unknown dangers of the Dover Barrage—but I have strayed from what I meant to write about—my first command and her crew.

The quarters in this class are immensely superior to the U.C.-boats. Here I have a little cabin to myself, with a knee-hole table in it. My First Lieutenant, the Navigator and the Engineer have bunks in a room together, and then we have a small officers' mess.

On this job up here, as we are not to return to Germany for supplies, and, consequently, I should say we may have to live on what we can get out of steamers, I don't propose to use my torpedoes unless I meet a warship or an exceptionally large steamer.

The gun's the thing, as Arnauld de la Perrière has proved in the Mediterranean; but half the fellows won't follow his example, simply because they don't realize that it's no use employing the gun unless it is used accurately, and good shooting only comes after long drill.

I have impressed this fact on my gun crew, and particularly the two gun-layers, and I make Voigtman (my young First Lieutenant) take the crew through their loading drill twice a day, together with practice of rapid manning of the gun after a "surface" or rapid abandonment of the gun should the diving alarms sound in the middle of practice. I have also impressed on Voigtman that I consider that he is the gun control officer, and that I expect him to make the efficient working of the gun his main consideration.

As regards the crew, they are the usual mixed crowd that one gets nowadays: half of them are old sailors, the others recruits and new arrivals from the Fleet. My main business at the moment is to get the youngsters into shape, and for this purpose I have been doing a number of crash dives. It also gives me an opportunity of getting used to the boat's peculiarities under water. She seems to have a tendency to become tail-heavy, but this may be due to bad trimming.

Voigtman has been in U.B.43 for nine months, and seems a capable officer. Socially, I don't think he can boast of much descent, but he has no airs, and treats me with pleasing respect, apart from service considerations.

* * * * *

A very awkward accident took place this morning, which resulted in severe injury to Johann Wiener, my second coxswain.

A party of men under his direction were engaged in shifting the stern torpedo from its tube, in order to replace it with a spare torpedo, as I never allow any of my torpedoes to stay in the tube for more than a week at a time owing to corrosion. The torpedo which had been in the tube had been launched back and was on the floor plates.

The spare torpedo, destined for the vacant tube, was hanging overhead, when without any warning the hook on the lifting band fractured, and the 1,000 kilogrammes' mass of metal crashed down.

Wonderful to relate, no one was killed, but two men were badly bruised, and Wiener has been very seriously injured. He was standing astride the spare torpedo, and his right leg was extremely badly crushed, mostly below the knee.

Unfortunately it took about ten minutes to release him from his position of terrible agony. I should have expected him to faint, but he did not. His face went dead white, and he began to sweat freely, but otherwise endured his ordeal with praiseworthy fortitude.

"The 1,000 kilogrammes of metal crashed down."

"Good-bye! Steer west for America!"

"It is a snug anchorage and here I intend to remain."

I am now confronted with a perplexing situation. I cannot take him back to Germany; I cannot even leave my station and proceed south to any of the Norwegian ports. If I could find a neutral steamer with a doctor on board, I would tranship him to her; but the chances of this God-send materializing are a thousand to one in these latitudes. If I sighted a hospital ship I would close her, but as far as I know at present there are no hospital ships running up here. The chances of outside assistance may therefore be reckoned as nil. Wiener's hope of life depends on me, and I cannot make up my mind to take the step which sooner or later must be taken—that is to say, amputation.

It is a curious fact, but true, nevertheless, that although, as a result of the war, men's lives, considered in quantity, seem of little importance, when it comes to the individual case, a personal contact, a man's life assumes all its pre-war importance.

I feel acutely my responsibility in this matter. I see from his papers that he is a married man with a family; this seems to make it worse. I feel that a whole chain of people depend on me.

* * * * *

Since I wrote the above words this morning, Wiener has taken a decided turn for the worse.

I have been reading the "Medical Handbook," with reference to the remarks on amputation, gangrene, etc., and I have also been examining his leg. The poor devil is in great pain, and there is no doubt that mortification has set in, as was indeed inevitable. I have decided that he must have his last chance, and that at 8 p.m. to-night I will endeavour to amputate.

Midnight.
I have done it—only partially successful.

* * * * *

Last night, in accordance with my decision, I operated on Wiener. Voigtman assisted me. It was a terrible business, but I think it desirable to record the details whilst they are fresh in my memory, as a Court of Inquiry may be held later on. Voigtman and I spent the whole afternoon in the study of such meagre details on the subject as are available in the

"Medical Handbook." We selected our knives and a saw and sterilized them; we also disinfected our hands.

At 7.45 I dived the boat to sixty metres, at which depth the boat was steady. We had done our best with the wardroom-table, and upon this the patient was placed. I decided to amputate about four inches above the knee, where the flesh still seemed sound. I considered it impracticable to administer an anaesthetic, owing to my absolute inexperience in this matter.

Three men held the patient down, as with a firm incision I began the work. The sawing through the bone was an agonizing procedure, and I needed all my resolution to complete the task. Up to this stage all had gone as well as could be expected, when I suddenly went through the last piece of bone and cut deep into the flesh on the other side. An instantaneous gush of blood took place, and I realized that I had unexpectedly severed the popliteal artery, before Voigtman, who was tying the veins, was ready to deal with it.

I endeavoured to staunch the deadly flow by nipping the vein between my thumb and forefinger, whilst Voigtman hastily tried to tie it. Thinking it was tied, I released it, and alas! the flow at once started again; once more I seized the vein, and once again Voigtman tried to tie it. Useless— we could not stop the blood. He would undoubtedly have bled to death before our eyes, had not Voigtman cauterized the place with an electric soldering-iron which was handy.

Much shaken, I completed the amputation, and we dressed the stump as well as we could.

At the moment of writing he is still alive, but as white as snow; he must have lost litres of blood through that artery.

9 p.m.

Wiener died two hours ago. I should say the immediate cause of death was shock and loss of blood. I did my best.

* * * * *

We have been out on this extended patrol area seven days, but not a wisp of smoke greets our eyes.

Nothing but sea, sea, sea. Oh, how monotonous it is! I cannot make out where the shipping has got to. Tomorrow I am going to close the North Cape again. I think everything must be going inside me. I am too far out here.

* * * * *

The North Cape bears due east. Nothing afloat in sight. Where the devil can all the shipping be? In ten days' time I am due to meet my supply ship; meanwhile I think I'll have to take another cast out, of three hundred miles or so.

* * * * *

Nothing in sight, nothing, nothing.

The barometer falling fast and we are in for a gale. I have decided to make the coast again, as I don't want to fail to turn up punctually at the rendezvous.

* * * * *

In the Standarak-Landholm Fjord—thank heavens.

Heavens! we have had a time. We were still two hundred and fifty miles from the coast when we were caught by the gale. And a gale up here is a gale, and no second thoughts about it. To say it blew with the force of ten thousand devils is to understate the case. The sea came on to us in huge foaming rollers like waves of attacking infantry intent on overwhelming us.

We struggled east at about three knots. But she stuck it magnificently. Low scudding clouds obscured the sky and came like a procession of ghosts from the north-east. Sun observations were impossible for two reasons. Firstly, no one could get on deck; secondly, there was no visible sun. This lasted for three days, at the end of which time we had only the vaguest idea as to where we were.

The gale then blew out, but, contrary to all expectations, was succeeded by a most abominable fog, thick and white like cotton-wool. These were hardly ideal conditions under which to close a rocky and unknown coast, but it had to be done. The trouble was that it was entirely useless taking soundings, as the twenty-metre depth-line on the chart went right up to the land. We crept slowly eastwards, till, when by dead reckoning we were ten miles inside the coast, the Navigator accidentally leant on the whistle lever; this action on his part probably saved the ship, as an immediate echo answered the blast. In an instant we were going full-speed astern. We altered course sixteen points and proceeded ten miles westerly, where we lay on and off the coast all night, cursing the fog.

Next day it lifted, and we spent the whole time trying to find the entrance to the S. Landholm Fjord. The coast appeared to bear no resemblance to the chart whatsoever.

The cliffs stand up to a height of several hundred metres, with occasional clefts where a stream runs down. There are no trees, houses, animals, or any signs of life, except sea birds, of which there are myriads. The Engineer declares he saw a reindeer, but five other people on deck failed to see any signs of the beast.

After hours of nosing about, during which my heart was in my mouth, as I quite expected to fetch up on a pinnacle rock, items which are officially described in the Handbook as being "very numerous," we rounded a bluff and got into a place which seems to answer the description of S. Landholm. At any rate, it is a snug anchorage, and here I intend to remain for a few days, and hope for my store-ship to turn up.

I've posted a daylight look-out on top of the bluff; it would be very awkward to be caught unawares in this place, which is only about 150 metres wide in places.

I'm taking advantage of the rest to give the crew some exercises and execute various minor repairs to the Diesels.

* * * * *

Yesterday we fought what must be one of the most remarkable single-ship actions of the war.

At 9 a.m. the look-out on the cliffs reported smoke to the northward.

I got the anchor up and made ready to push off, but still kept the look-out ashore. At 9.30 he reported a destroyer in sight, which seemed serious if she chose to look into my particular nook.

At any rate, I thought, I wouldn't be caught like a rat, so I got my look-out on board—a matter of ten minutes—and then proceeded out, trimmed down and ready for diving.

When I drew clear of the entrance I saw the enemy distant about a thousand metres. I at once recognized her as being one of the oldest type of Russian torpedo boats afloat. When I established this fact, a devil entered into my mind, and did a most foolhardy act.

I decided that I would not retreat beneath the sea, but that I would fight her as one service ship to another.

When I make up my mind, I do so in no uncertain manner—indecision is abhorrent to me—and I sharply ordered, "Gun's Crew—Action."

I can still see the comical look of wonderment which passed over my First Lieutenant's face, but he knows me, and did not hesitate an instant. We drilled like a battleship, and in sixty-five seconds—I timed it as a matter of interest—from my order we fired the first shot. It fell short.

Extraordinary to relate, the torpedo boat, without firing a gun, put her helm hard over, and started to steam away at her full speed, which I suppose was about seventeen knots.

I actually began to chase her—a submarine chasing a torpedo boat! It was ludicrous.

With broad smiles on their faces, my good gun's crew rapidly fired the gun, and we had the satisfaction of striking her once, near her after funnel, but it did no vital damage, as a few minutes afterwards she drew out of range! What a pack of incompetent cowards!

They never fired a shot at us. I suppose half of them were drunk or else in a state of semi-mutiny, for one hears strange tales of affairs in Russia these days.

The whole incident was quite humorous, but I realized that I had hardly been wise, as without doubt the English will hear of this, and these trawlers of theirs will turn up, and I'm certainly not going to try any heroics with John Bull, who is as tough a fighter as we are.

Meanwhile, what of the supply ship, for I'm supposed to meet her here, and it's already twenty-four hours since yesterday's epoch-making battle and I expect the English any moment.

* * * * *

My doubts were removed for me since I received special orders at noon by high-power wireless from Nordreich, and on decoding them found that, for some reason or other, we are ordered to proceed to Muckle Flugga Cape, and thence down the coast of Shetlands to the Fair Island Channel, where we are directed to cruise till further orders. Special warning is included as to encountering friendly submarines.

It appears to me that a special concentration of U-boats is being ordered round about the Orkneys, and that some big scheme is on hand.

We are now steering south-westerly to make Muckle Flugga, which I hope to do in four days' time if the weather holds.

These Northern waters have proved very barren of shipping in the last few weeks, and this fact, coupled with the approaching winter weather, which must be fiendish in these latitudes, makes me quite ready to exchange the Archangel billet for the work round the Orkneys and Shetlands, though this is damnable enough in the winter, in all conscience.

There is only one fly in the ointment, and that is that this premature return to North Sea waters might conceivably mean a visit to Zeebrugge, though this class are not likely to be sent there.

Though it is many weeks since I left Zoe, I have not been able to forget her. I continually wonder what she is doing, and often when I am not on my guard she wanders into my thoughts.

Whilst I am up here, it does not matter much, except that it causes me unhappiness, but if I found myself at Bruges it would be very hard. However, I don't suppose I shall ever see her again.

* * * * *

Sighted Muckle Flugga this morning, and shaped course for Fair Island.

* * * * *

Oh! what a hell I have passed through. I can hardly realize that I am alive, but I am, though whether I shall be to-morrow morning is doubtful—it all depends on the weather, and who would willingly stake their life on North Sea weather at this time of the year?

Curses on the man who sent us to the Fair Island Channel. Where the devil is our Intelligence Service? If we make Flanders I have a story to tell that will open their eyes, blind bats that they are, luxuriating in the comfort of their fat staff jobs ashore.

The Fair Island Channel is an English death-trap; it stinks with death. By cursed luck we arrived there just as the English were trying one of their new devices, and it is the devil. Exactly what the system is, I don't quite know, and I hope never again to have to investigate it.

For forty-seven, hours we have been hunted like a rat, and now, with the pressure hull leaking in three places, and the boat half full of chlorine, we are struggling back on the surface, practically incapable of diving at least for more than ten minutes at a time. Even on the surface, with all the fans working, one must wear a gas mask to penetrate the fore compartment. Oh! these English, what devils they are!

Here is what happened:

Fair Island was away on our port beam when we sighted a large English trawler, which I suspected of being a patrol. To be on the safe side, I dived and proceeded at twenty metres for about an hour.

At 5 p.m. (approximately) I came up to periscope depth to have a look round, but quickly dived again as I discovered a trawler, steering on the same course as myself, about a thousand metres astern of me. This was the more disconcerting, as in the short time at my disposal it seemed to me that she was remarkably similar to the craft I had seen in the afternoon, and yet this hardly seemed likely, as I did not think she could have sighted me then.

On diving, I altered course ninety degrees, and proceeded for half an hour at full speed, then altered another ninety degrees, in the same direction as the previous alteration, and diving to thirty metres I proceeded at dead slow. By midnight I had been diving so much that I decided to get a charge on the batteries before dawn; I also wanted to be up at 1 a.m. to make my position report.

I surfaced after a good look round through the right periscope, which, as usual, revealed nothing. I had hardly got on the bridge, when a flash of flame stabbed the night on the starboard beam and a shell moaned just overhead.

I crash-dived at once, but could not get under before the enemy fired a second shot at us, which fortunately missed us. As we dived I ordered the helm hard a starboard, to counteract the expected depth-charge attack. We must have been a hundred and fifty metres from the first charge and a little below it, five others followed in rapid succession, but were further away, and we suffered no damage beyond a couple of broken lights. The situation was now extremely unpleasant. I did not dare venture to the surface, and thus missed my 1 a.m. signal from Headquarters. I wanted a charge badly, and so proceeded at the lowest possible speed. At regular intervals our enemy dropped one depth-charge somewhere astern of us, but these reports always seemed the same distance away.

At dawn I very cautiously came up to periscope depth, and had a look. To my consternation I discovered our relentless pursuer about 1,500 metres away on the port quarter. In some extraordinary manner he had tracked us during the night.

I dived and altered course through ninety degrees to south.

At 9 a.m. a tremendous explosion shook the boat from stem to stern, smashing several lights, and giving her a big inclination up by the bow.

As I was only at twenty metres I feared the boat would break surface, and our enemy was evidently very nearly right over us. I at once ordered hard to dive, and went down to the great depth of ninety-five metres.

A series of shattering explosions somewhere above us showed that we were marked down, and we were only saved from destruction by our great depth, the English charges being set apparently to about thirty metres.

At noon the situation was critical in the extreme. My battery density was down to 1,150, the few lamps that I had burning were glowing with a faint, dull red appearance, which eloquently told of the falling voltage and the dying struggles of the battery.

The motors with all fields out were just going round. The faces of the crew, pallid with exhaustion, seemed of an ivory whiteness in the dusky gloom of the boat, which never resembled a gigantic and fantastically ornamental coffin so closely as she did at that time.

The air was fetid. I struck a match; it went out in my fingers. The slightest effort was an agony. I bent down to take off my sea-boots, and cold sweat dropped off my forehead, and my pulse rose with a kind of jerk to a rapid beating, like a hammer.

I left one sea-boot on.

At 1 p.m. a deputation of the crew came aft, and in whispered voices implored me to surface the boat and make a last effort on the surface. A muffled report, as our implacable enemy dropped a depth-charge somewhere astern of us, added point to the conversation, and showed me that our appearance on the surface could have but one end.

At 3 p.m. the second coxswain, who was working the hydroplanes, fell off his stool in a dead faint.

At 3.30 p.m. the supreme crisis was reached: two more men fainted, and I realized that if I did not surface at once I might find the crew incapable of starting the Diesels.

At the order "Surface," a feeble cheer came from the men.

We surfaced, and I dragged myself-up to the conning tower. Luckily we started the Diesels with ease, and in a few minutes gusts of beautiful air were circulating through the boat.

Meanwhile, what of the enemy? I had half expected a shell as soon as we came up, and it was with great anxiety that I looked round. We had been slightly favoured by fortune in that the only thing in sight was a trawler away on the port beam. It was our hunter.

I trimmed right down, hoping to avoid being seen, as it was essential to stay on the surface and get some amperes into the battery. I also altered course away from him.

It was about 5 p.m. that I saw two trawlers ahead, one on each bow. By this time the boat's crew had quite recovered, but I did not wish to dive, as the battery was still pitiably low. I gradually altered course to north-east, but after half an hour's run I almost ran on top of a group of patrols in the dusk.

I crash-dived, and they must have seen me go down, as a few minutes later the boat was violently shaken by a depth-charge.

We were at twenty metres, still diving at the time. I consulted the chart, but could find no bottoming ground within fifty miles, a distance which was quite beyond my powers.

At 11 p.m. I simply had to come up again and get a charge on the batteries.

From 7 p.m. to 10 p.m., at regular half-hourly intervals, a depth-charge had gone off somewhere within a radius of two miles of me. Needless to say, I was only crawling along at about one knot and altering course frequently. What was so terrible was the patent fact that the patrols in this area had evidently got some device which enabled them to keep in continual touch with me to a certain extent.

These monotonous and regular depth-charges seemed to say: "We know, Oh! U-boat, that we are somewhere near you, and here is a depth-charge just to tell you that we haven't lost you yet."[17]

As an hour had elapsed since the last depth-charge, I felt fairly happy at coming up, and on making the surface I was delighted to find a pitch-black night and a considerable sea. From 10 p.m. to 1 a.m. I actually had three hours of peace, and in this period I managed to cram a considerable amount of stuff into the batteries. The densities were rising nicely and all seemed well, when I did what I now see was a very foolish thing.

I made my 1 a.m. wireless report to Nordreich, in which I requested orders at 3 a.m. and reported my position, together with the fact that I had been badly hunted.

In twenty-five minutes they were on me again! I had most idiotically assumed that the English had no directional wireless in these parts. They have. They've got everything that they have ever tried up there; it was concentrated in that infernal Fair Island Channel.

I was only saved by seeing a destroyer coming straight at me, silhouetted against, the low-lying crescent of a new moon. When I dived she was about six hundred metres away. As I have confessed to doing a foolish thing, I give myself the pleasure of recording a cleverer move on my part. I anticipated depth-charge attack as a matter of course, but instead of going down to twenty-five metres, I kept her at twelve.

---

17 Karl was quite right; it is evident that he had the misfortune to encounter one of our new hydrophone-hunting groups, just started In the Fair Island Channel. The incident of the depth-charges every half-hour was known as "Tickling up." Probably the patrol only heard faint noises from him.—ETIENNE.

The depth-charges came all right, seven smashing explosions, but, as I had calculated, they were set to go off at about thirty metres, and so were well below me.

The boat was thrown bodily up by one, and I think the top of the conning tower must have broken surface, but there was little danger of this being seen in the prevailing water conditions.

* * * * *

I have just had to stop recording my experiences of the past forty-eight hours, as the Navigator, who is on watch, sent down a message to say that smoke was in sight.

The next hour was full of anxiety, but by hauling off to port we managed to lose it. I then had a little food, and I will now conclude my account before trying again to get some sleep.

The account continued.

All my hopes of getting up again that night, both for the purpose of charging and of getting the 3 a.m. signal, were doomed to be disappointed, as the hydrophone operator kept on reporting the noise of destroyers overhead. Occasional distant thuds seemed to indicate a never-ending supply of depth-charges, but they were about four or five miles from me. Perhaps some other unfortunate devil was going through the fires of hell.

At daylight on the second day my position was still miserable. The battery was getting low again, the sea had gone down, and when I put my periscope up at 9 a.m. the horizon seemed to be ringed with patrols. I felt as if I was in an invisible net, and though I endeavoured to conceal my apprehension from the crew, I could see from the listless way they went about their duties that they realized that once again we were near the end of our resources.

All the forenoon we crept along at thirty metres, until the tension was broken at 1 p.m. by a furious depth-charge attack. In some extraordinary way they had located me again and closed in upon me. The first charges were some little distance off, and as they got closer a feeling of desperation overcame me, and I seriously contemplated ending the agony by surfacing and fighting to the last with my gun.

Curiously enough, the procedure that I adopted was the exact opposite. I decided to dive deep. I went down to 114 metres. At this exceptional depth, three rivets in the pressure hull began to leak, and jets of water with the rigidity of bars of iron shot into the boat. I held on for five minutes, which was sufficient to save me from the depth-charge attack, though two which went off almost above me broke some lamps. I then came up to twenty metres and slowly crawled on. Throughout the long afternoon, though we were not directly attacked again, I heard depth-charges on several occasions sufficiently close to me to demonstrate that these implacable and tireless devils had an idea of the area I was in.

By a supreme effort, working one motor at the only speed it would go, viz., "Dead slow," I managed to squeeze out the battery until I estimated it must be dusk.

There was only one thing to do—I surfaced. It was not as dark as I had hoped, and I saw a fairly large sloop-like vessel, about eight thousand metres away, on the port beam. She must have seen me simultaneously, as the flash of a gun darted from her, the shell falling short.

I couldn't dive; there seemed only one thing to do: fight and then die. I ordered the gun's crew up, and the unequal duel began. We were going full speed on the Diesels, and my course was east by north. A good deal of water and spray was flying over the gun, and my crew had little hope of doing much accurate shooting, but I have often found that when one is being fired at there is nothing so comforting as the sound of one's own gun.

Our enemy was armed with two large guns, fifteen centimetres or over, but had no speed, a discovery which raised my hopes again. It was soon evident that, provided we were not heading for another patrol, if we could survive ten minutes' shelling, we should be saved for the time being by the fading light, which was evidently causing our enemy increasing difficulties, as his shots alternated between very short and very much over.

I was actually congratulating the Navigator on our escape, and I had just told the gun's crew to cease firing at the blurred outlines on the port quarter from which the random shells still came, when there was a sheet of yellow flame and a jar which threw me against the signalman. The latter had been standing near the conning-tower hatch, and unfortunately I knocked him off his balance, and he fell with a thud into the upper conning tower. He had the good fortune to escape with a couple of ribs broken, but when I recovered myself and got to my feet, far worse consequences met my eyes.

By the worst of ill-luck, a shell which must have been fired practically at random had hit the gun just below the port trunnion.

The result of the explosion was very severe. Four of the seven men at the gun had been blown overboard, the breech worker was uninjured, though from the way he swayed about it was evident that he was dazed, and I expected to see him fall over the side at any moment. The remaining two men were as dead as horse-flesh.

The material damage was even more serious. The gun had been practically thrown out of its cradle, but in the main the trunnion blocks had held firm, and the whole pedestal had been carried over to starboard.

The really terrible effects of this injury were not apparent at first sight, but I soon realized them, for an hour later (we had shaken off the sloop) I saw red flame on the horizon, which plainly indicated flaming at the funnel from some destroyer doubtless looking for us at high speed.

I dived, intending to surface again as soon as possible. With this intention in my head, I did not go below the upper conning tower. We had barely got to ten metres, when loud cries from below and the disquieting noise of rushing water told me that something was wrong. I blew all tanks, surfaced, left the First Lieutenant on watch and went below.

There were five centimetres of water on the battery boards, and I understood at once that we could never dive again.

For the pedestal of the gun, in being forced over, had strained the longitudinal seam of the pressure hull, to which it is bolted, and a shower of water had come through as soon as we got under.

It might have been hoped that this was enough, but no! our cup was not yet full. Chlorine gas suddenly began to fill the fore-end. The salt water running down into the battery tanks had found acid, and though I ordered quantities of soda to be put down into the tank, it became, and still is at the moment of writing, impossible to move forward of the conning tower without putting on a gas mask and oxygen helmet. So we are helpless, and at the mercy of any little trawler, or even the weather.

We have no gun; we cannot dive. The English must know that they have hit us, and every hour I expect to see the hull of a destroyer climb over the horizon astern.

We are fortunate in two respects: in that for the time being the weather seems to promise well, and our Diesels are thoroughly sound.

We are ordered to Zeebrugge—I could have wished elsewhere for many reasons, but it does not matter, as I cannot believe we are intended to escape.

I feel I would almost welcome an enemy ship, it would soon be over; but this uncertainty and anxiety drags on for hour after hour—and now I cannot sleep, though I haven't slept properly for over seventy hours. I am so worn out that my body screams for sleep, but it is denied to me, and so, lest I go mad, I write; it is better to do this, though my eyes ache and the letters seem to wriggle, than to stand up on the bridge looking for the smoke of our enemies, or to lie in my bunk and count the revolutions of the Diesels; thousands of thousands of thudding beats, one after the other, relentless hammer strokes.

I have endured much.

NOTE BY ETIENNE
A break occurs in Karl von Schenk's diary at this juncture. Fortunately the main outlines of the story are preserved owing to Zoe's long letter, which

was in a small packet inside the cover of the second notebook. Zoe's letter will be reproduced in this book in its proper chronological position, but in order to save the reader the trouble of reading the book from the letter back to this point, a brief summary of what took place is given here. The entries in his diary which follow the words "I have endured much," are very meagre for a period which seems to have been about a month in length. There is no further mention of the latter stages of Karl's passage in the wrecked boat to Zeebrugge, so it is presumed that he made that port without further adventure. He was evidently on the verge of a nervous breakdown, and appears to have been suffering from very severe insomnia. He had been hunted for two days, during which he was perpetually on the verge of destruction, and the cumulative effect of such an experience is bound to leave its mark on the strongest man. When he got back to Zeebrugge he must have been at the end of his tether, and whether by chance or design it was when Karl was, as he would have said, "at a low mental ebb" that Zoe made her last and successful attack upon his resolution not to see her again unless she consented to marry him. It is plain from her letter that when he left her after the stormy interview in which he vowed never to see her again, Zoe did not lose hope. She seems to have kept herself au courant with his movements, and actually to have known when he was expected in.

We know that she had many friends amongst the officers, and it is probable that from one of these she was able to get information about Karl's movements.

Bruges was probably a hot-bed of U-boat gossip, and, not unlike the conditions at certain other Naval ports during the war, the ladies were often too well informed. At any rate it appears that Zoe rushed to see Karl directly he arrived at Bruges, and found him a mental and physical wreck, suffering from acute insomnia.

With the impetuous vigour which evidently guided most of her actions, she took complete charge of Karl, and, as he was due for four days' leave, she whisked him off to the forest.

Karl may have protested, but was probably in no state to wish to do so. At her shooting-box in the forest Zoe achieved her desire, and the stubborn *struggle between the lovers ended in victory for the woman. There is an entry in Karl's diary which may refer to this period; he simply says, "Slept at last! Oh, what a joy!"*

If this entry was written in the forest, it seemed as if Karl had been unable to sleep until Zoe carried him off to the forest peace of her shooting-box and surrounded him with the atmosphere of her tender sympathy.

There is no evidence of the light in which Karl viewed his defeat, when, having regained his strength, he was able to take stock of the changed situation. It is reasonable to suppose that his silence upon this matter in the pages of his diary is evidence that he was ashamed of what he must have considered a great act of weakness on his part.

At all events he realized that he had crossed the Rubicon and that he had better acquiesce in the fait accompli.

He seems to have been in harbour for about six weeks, during which he lived with Zoe, and the lovers enjoyed a brief spell of happiness before Karl set out on his next trip.

Karl seems to have found those six weeks very pleasant ones, though his diary merely contains brief references, such as: "A. day in the country with Z."; "Z. and I went to the Cavalry dance," and other trivial entries—of his thoughts there is not a word.

About the end of 1917 Karl's boat was repaired, and he left for the Atlantic; and once more resumed full entries in his diary.

ETIENNE.

Karl's Diary resumed.

Sailed at 9 p.m. last night, and we are now seventeen miles off Beachy Head. The Straits of Dover were frightful; the glare of the acetylene flares on the barrage showed for miles. Seen from a distance it gave me the impression of the gates of hell, through which we had to pass.

I dived, ten miles away, and went through with the tide at a depth of forty metres.

Two hours and three quarters of suspense, and at dawn we came up, having passed safely through the great deathtrap. At the moment there is nothing in sight, except a little smoke on the horizon. I am going to dive again till dusk.

2 a.m.

We are thrashing down the Channel with a south-westerly wind right ahead. My instructions are to work for two days between the Lizard and Kinsale Head, and then proceed far out in the Atlantic, where the convoys are supposed to meet the destroyers.

That Fair Island Channel experience was enough for a lifetime. Death, quick, short and sudden, this I am ready for. But torture, slow, long and drawn-out, is not in the bargain which in this year of grace every civilized man and half the savages of the world seem to have had to make with the god Mars.

As I sit in this steel, cigar-shaped mass of machinery, the question rings incessantly in my ears: "To what object is all this war directed, when analysed from the point of view of the individual?"

It does not satisfy any longing of mine. I have not got a lust for battle: no one who fights has a lust for battle. Editors of newspapers and people on General Staffs, possibly also Cabinet Ministers, have lusts for battles, as long as they arrange the battle and talk about it afterwards—curse them!

The only thing I want is to be with Zoe. I want to live and spend long years with her, enjoying life—this life of which I have spent half already, and now perhaps it will be taken from me by some other man: some Englishman who doesn't really want to take my life, reckoned as an individual.

Around me in the darkness are the patrol boats, manned by the Englishmen who are seeking my life. Seeking it, not to gratify their private emotions, but because we are all in the whirlpool of War and cannot escape.

Like an avalanche, it seems to gather strength and speed as it rolls on, this War of Nations. The world must be mad! I cannot see how it can ever stop. England will never be defeated at sea. We shall conquer on land—then what?

An inconclusive peace.

Even if we smash this island Empire and gain the dominion of the world, how will it advantage me? I can see no way in which I can gain.

It would be said, if any one should read this: *Gott!* what a selfish point of view—he thinks only of his personal gain, not of his country.

But, confound it all, I reply, answer me this:

Do I exist for my country, or does my country exist for me?

For example, does man live for the sake of the Church, or was the Church created for man?

Does not my country exist for my benefit?

Surely it is so.

Then again, I am risking my all, my life; I live in danger, apprehension and great discomfort; I do all these things, and yet if as a reasonable man I ponder what advantage I am to gain from all these sacrifices I am adjudged selfish.

It is all madness; I cannot fathom the meaning of these things.

* * * * *

In position on the Bristol line of approach, the weather is bad.

At twenty metres.

Once again Death has stretched forth his bony fingers to catch me by the throat, and only by a chance have I wriggled free.

Yesterday afternoon at 5 p.m. we sighted a small steamer flying Spanish colours and steering for Cardiff. The weather was choppy, but not too bad, and I decided to exercise the gun's crew, though I did not think there would be much doing, as the Spaniards soon give in.

I opened fire at six thousand metres, and pitched a shell ahead of her and ran up the signal to heave-to. The wretched little craft paid no attention, and continued on her lumbering course. I suspected the presence of an Englishman on her bridge, and determined to hit.

This we did with our sixth shot, and she stopped dead and wallowed in the trough, with clouds of steam pouring out of her engine-room; we had evidently got the engine-room.

As we closed her, it was evident that a tremendous panic was taking place on board. The port sea boat was being launched, but one fall broke and the occupants fell into the water. My Navigator begged me to give her another, which I did, and hit her right aft. Two boatloads of gesticulating individuals now appeared from the shelter of her lee side and began pulling wildly away from the ship.

The Navigator, whose eyes were dancing with excitement, was very keen to play with them by spraying the water with machine-gun bullets; but it seemed to me to be waste of ammunition, and I would not permit it.

Meanwhile we had approached to within about four hundred metres of her port bow. I was debating whether to accelerate her sinking, when I noticed that a fire had broken out aft, and I became possessed with a childish curiosity to see the fire being put out as she sank. It was a kind of contest between the elements.

As I watched her, I was startled to hear three or four reports from the region of the fire.

"Ammunition!" shouted the pilot, with wide-opened eyes.

In an instant I pressed the diving alarm as I realized our deadly peril. Fool that I had been, she was a decoy-ship. They must have realized on board that I had seen through their disguise, for as we began to move forward, under the motors, a trap-door near her bows fell down, the white ensign was broken at the fore, and a 4-inch gun opened fire from the embrasure that was revealed on her side.

We were fortunate in that our conning tower was already right ahead of the enemy, and as I dropped down into the conning tower, I saw that as she could not turn we were safe.

A few shells plunged harmlessly into the water near our stern, and then we were under.

We came up to a periscope depth, and I surveyed her from a position off her stern. She was sinking fast, but I felt so furious at being nearly trapped that I could not resist giving her a torpedo; detonation was complete, and a mass of wreckage shot into the air as the hull of the ship disappeared. As to the two boats, I left them to make the best course to land that they could.

As they were fifty miles off the shore when I left them and it blew force six a few hours afterwards, I rather think they have joined the list of "Missing." We are now steering due west to our second position.

* * * * *

Received orders last night to return to base forthwith on the north about route.[18]

I have shaped course to pass fifty miles north of Muckle Flugga; no more Fair Island Channel for me.

* * * * *

Statlandlet in sight, with the Norwegian coast looking very lovely under the snow—we never saw a ship from north of the Shetlands to this place, when we saw a light cruiser of the town class steaming south-west at high speed.

---

18 This means into the North Sea round Scotland.—

She had probably been on patrol off this place, where the Inner and Outer Leads join up and ships have to leave the three-mile limit.

She was well away from me, and an attack would have been useless. I did not shed any tears; I have lost much of the fire-eating ideas which filled my mind when I first joined this service.

* * * * *

We are due off the mole at 8 p.m. tonight, and my heart leaps with joy at the thought of seeing my Zoe; already I can almost imagine her lovely arms round my neck, her face raised to mine, and all the other wonderful things that make her so glorious in my eyes.

NOTE BY ETIENNE

Before quoting the next entry in Karl's journal it is necessary to explain the situation which confronted him when he arrived in Zeebrugge. In his absence, his beloved Zoe had been arrested as an Allied Agent, and she was tried for espionage within a day or two of his arrival. There is no record of how he heard the news, and the blow he sustained was probably so terrible that whilst there was yet hope he felt no desire to write; but, as will be seen, there came a time when he turned to his journal as the last friend that remained to him. It is a curious fact that, with the exception of an entry at the beginning of this journal, Karl makes little mention of his mother and home at Frankfurt. Though he does not say so, it seems possible that his mother had heard of his entanglement with Zoe, and a barrier had risen between them; this suggestion gains strength from the fact that in his blackest moments of despair he never seems to consider the question of turning to Frankfurt for sympathy. Interest is naturally aroused as to the details of Zoe's trial. The available material consists solely of the long letter she wrote to him from Bruges jail. It may be that one day the German archives of the period of occupation will reveal further details. Information on the subject is possibly at the disposal of the British Intelligence Service, but this would be kept secret. All we know on the matter is derived from the letter, which has been preserved inside the second volume of Karl's diary.

There seems no doubt that she was caught red-handed, but to say more would be to anticipate her own words.

It was a matter of some difficulty to know where best to introduce Zoe's letter, but with a view to securing as much continuity of thought in the story as possible it has been decided to quote it at this juncture, although he did not receive it until after he had made the entry in the journal which will be quoted directly after the letter.

I would like to appeal to any reader who may happen to be engaged in administrative or reconstructive work in Belgium, to communicate with me, care of Messrs. Hutchinson, should he handle any papers dealing with Zoe's trial.

ETIENNE.

ZOE'S LETTER

MY BEST BELOVED,

When you get this letter cease to sorrow for what will have happened, for I shall be at rest, and in peace at last, freed from a world in which I have known bitter sorrow and, until you came into my life, but little joy.

For these past months I am grateful to God, if such a being exists and regulates the conduct of a world gone mad.

For in a few hours I am to die.

It is harder for you than for me; one moment of agony I suffered, a moment that seemed to last a century, when, amidst the sea of faces that swam in a confused mass before me at the trial, I saw your eyes and the torture that you were suffering. When I saw your eyes I knew that the President had said I must die. I am glad that I was told this by you, the only one amongst all these men who loved me. I suppose the President spoke; I never heard him, but I saw your eyes and I knew.

My darling, it was cruel of you to come, cruel to me and cruel to yourself, but I loved you for being there; it showed me that up till the last you would stand by me, and until you read this you cannot know all the facts. That to you, as to the others, I must have seemed a woman spy and that nevertheless you stood by me, is to me a recollection of unsurpassable sweetness, compared with which all other thoughts of you fade into insignificance.

Know now, oh, well beloved, that I was not unworthy of your love.

I have a story to tell you, and I have such a little time left that I must write quickly. The priest who has been with me comes again an hour before the dawn, and he has promised to deliver these my last words of love into your hands.

My real name is Zoe Xenia Olga Sbeiliez, and I was born twenty-nine years ago at my father's country house at Inkovano, near Koniesfol. I am Polish; at least, my father was, and my mother comes from the Don country. There was a day when my father's ancestors were Princes in Poland. Poor Poland was torn by the vultures of Europe, just as your countrymen, my Karl, are tearing poor Belgium and France, and so my family lost estates year by year, and my grandfather is buried somewhere in the dreary steppes of Siberia because he dared to be a Polish patriot.

My father bowed before the storm, and under my mother's influence he never became mixed up with politics. Thus he lived on his estates at Inkovano, and nursed them for my younger brother, Alexandrovitch, the child of his old age. Alex would be nineteen now, had he lived. The estates were large as these things go in Western Europe, but they were but a garden as compared with the lands held by my great-grandfather, Boris Sbeiliez.

My father had a dream, and he dreamed this dream from the day Alex was born to the day they both died in each other's arms.

My father dreamt that one day the Tsars would soften their heart to Poland, and raise her up from the dust to a place amongst the nations, and my father dreamt that Alexandrovitch Sbeiliez would become a leader of Poland, as his ancestors had been before him. And so my father nursed his estates and pinched and saved, in preparation for the day when his beautiful dream should come true.

"A trapdoor near her bows fell down, the White Ensign was broken at the fore, and a 4-inch gun opened fire from the embrasure that was revealed on her side."

"I sighted two convoys, but there were destroyers there..."

My poor idealistic father never realized, oh, my Karl, that when one wants a thing one must fight—to the death. Alex was the apple of his eye, but I was much loved by my mother; perhaps she dreamed a dream about me—I know not, but she determined that I should have all that was necessary. Paris, Berlin, Munich, Dresden, and a season in London, then I came home at twenty-one, perfectly educated according to the world, beautiful according to men, and dressed according to Paris. But I was only to find out how little I knew. My mother and I used to take a house in Warsaw for the season, and I met many notable men and women. In these days I, also, thought I could do something for Poland, but after two or three seasons I found that I, too, was only dreaming idle dreams. Oh! my beloved, beware of dreaming idle dreams.

Listen! I once met the Prime Minister of all Russia at a reception. I captivated him, and thought, now! now! I shall do something.

I sat next to him at dinner; I talked of Poland—and I knew my subject—I talked brilliantly; he listened, he hung on my words, and he, the Prime Minister of all Russia, the Tsar's right-hand man, asked me to drive with him next day in his sledge. I, an almost unknown Polish girl!

When I accepted, I was in the seventh heaven of delight.

Next day he called and we set forth; at a deserted spot in the woods near Warsaw he tried to kiss me—I struck him in the face with the butt of his own whip.

That was why he had hung on my words, that was why he had taken me for my drive; it was my Polish body that interested *him*—not Poland.

The Prime Minister of Russia was confined to his room for two days, "owing to an indisposition." How I laughed when I saw the bulletin in the paper, signed by two doctors, but it taught me a lesson; I never dreamt idle dreams again.

No, I am wrong, my beloved. I dreamt an idle dream, a lovely dream about you and I. An after-the-war dream, if this war should ever end, but like other dreams it has ended—in dreams.

But I must hurry, for my little watch tells me that one hour of my five has gone, and I have much to say.

I could have married, and married brilliantly, but Poland held me back. I did not know what I could do for my country, it all seemed so hopeless, and yet I felt that perhaps one day . . . and I felt I ought to be single when that day came.

It was not easy, my Karl, sometimes it was hard; one man there was, Sergius was his Christian name; he loved me madly, and sometimes I thought—but no matter, he is dead now, killed at Tannenberg, and I—well, I will tell you more of my story.

When the war broke out and clouded over that last beautiful summer in 1914 (I wonder will there ever be another like it in your lifetime, my Karl? No, I don't think it can ever be quite the same after all this!), we were all in the country. Alex was back from his school in Petrograd, and my father kept him at home for the autumn term.

How well I remember the excitement, the mobilization, the blessing of the colours, the wave of patriotism which swept over the country; even I, under the influence of the specious proclamations that were issued broadcast by the Government, with their promises of reform, and redress for Poland after the war was over, felt more Russian than Polish. Lies! Lies! Lies! that was what the Government promises were, my Karl.

Under the stress of war the rottenness of that great whited sepulchre, Russia, feared the revival of the Polish spirit; it might have been awkward, and so they lied with their tongues in their cheeks, and we simple Poles believed them; the peasantry flocked to their depots, little knowing whom they fought, but the proclamations which were read to them told them they fought for Poland, and we women worked and prayed for the success of Russian arms.

Then the tide of war swept westward, and all day long and every day the troops, and the guns and the motor-cars and the wagons rolled through the village to the west.

Guarded hints in the papers seemed to say that all was not well in France, but France was so far away, and all the time the Russians were going west through our village. Mighty Russia was putting forth her strength, and the Austrian debacle was in full swing; these were great days, my Karl, for a Russian!

Then one day the long columns of men and all the traffic seemed to hesitate in the sluggish westward flow, and then it stopped, and then it began to go east. The weeks went on, and one day, very, very faintly, there was a rumbling like a distant thunderstorm. It was the guns! The front was coming back.

Have you ever seen forest fires, my Karl? We had them every autumn in our woods. If you have, then you know how all the small animals and the birds, the rabbits and the foxes, and perhaps a wolf or two, and the deer, and the thrushes and the linnets come out from the shelter of the trees, fleeing blindly from the great peril, anxious only to save their lives. So it was when the front came back. Herds of moujiks, the old men, the women, the children, the poor little babies, struggled blindly eastwards through the village.

Pushing their miserable household gods on handcarts, or staggering along with loads on their backs, and weary children dragging at their arms, the human tide flowed eastwards, round our house, begged perhaps a drink of water, and then wandered feverishly onwards.

They knew not in ninety-nine cases out of a hundred where they were going; their only destination was summed up in the words, "Away from the Front"—away from the ominous rumbling which began to get louder, away from that western horizon which was beginning to have a lurid glow at nights, like a sunset prolonged to dawn.

Then, as the Germans advanced more and more, the character of the tide changed, the civilian element was outnumbered by the military. Companies, battalions, brigades, sometimes in good order, sometimes in no order, marched through the village. They would often halt for a short time, and the officers would come up to the house, where my mother and I gave them what we could. My father lived amongst his books and accounts, and bemoaned the extravagance of the war. Then there were the deserters, the stragglers, the walking wounded, the—but you know, my Karl, what an army in retreat means.

I must proceed with my story, for time moves relentlessly on.

One day a desperately wounded officer, a young Lieutenant of the Guard, a boy of twenty-five, was taken out of a motor ambulance to die.

The ambulance had stopped opposite our gates, and lying on his stretcher he had seen our garden, my garden. He knew he was to die, and he had begged with tears in his eyes to the doctor that he might be left in the garden.

Who could refuse him?

He died within two hours, amongst our flowers, with Alex and I at his side.

Before he died, he begged us, implored us, almost ordered us, to move east before it was too late.

We repeated his arguments to my father, but the latter was obdurate, and he swore that a regiment of angels would not move him from his ancestral home. So we made up our minds to stay.

Things got worse and worse, and one day shells fell in the grounds and we hid in the cellars. That night all our servants ran away, and my father cursed them for cowards. Next day in the early morning we heard machine guns fire outside the village, and then all was still.

At six o'clock Alex, white-faced, came running into the house. He had been down to the gates and he had seen the enemy. They were drunk, he said, and going down the street firing the houses and shooting the people as they came out.

It seemed impossible and yet it was true. It was growing dark, when we heard shouts and saw lights, and from the top of the house I saw a crowd of singing and shouting soldiers, with pine torches, half running, half walking up the drive.

They massed in a body opposite the house. Paralysed with terror, I looked down on the scene, and shuddered to see that every second man seemed to have a bottle. One of them fired a shot at the house, and next I remember a flood of light on the drive, and, in the circle of light, my father standing with hand raised. What my father intended can never be known, for, as he paused and faced the mob, a solitary shot rang out, and he fell in a huddled heap.

As he fell, a boyish voice from the door shouted "Murderers!" It was Alex. With his little pistol I had given him for a birthday present in his hand, he ran forward and, standing over my father's body, head thrown back, he pointed his pistol at the mob and fired twice. A man dropped, there was a flash of steel, the crowd surged forward, and—and, oh! my Karl, they had murdered my beloved brother, my darling Alex.

The next moment they were in the house. I escaped from my window on to the roof of the dairy, and from there down a water-pipe, across the yard to an old hay-loft. For a long time they ran in and out of the house, like ants, looting and pillaging; then there was a great shout, and for some time not a soul came out of the house. I guessed they had got into the cellars. At about midnight I saw that the house was on fire. In a few minutes it was an inferno and the drunken soldiers came pouring out, firing their rifles in all directions.

I had found a piece of rope in the loft. One end I placed on a hook and the other round my neck. I was close to the upper doors of the loft, with a drop to the courtyard, and thus I stayed, for I feared that some soldier, more sober than the rest, might explore the outhouses and find me. I was watching this unearthly spectacle, and never, my best beloved, did I conceive that man could become lower than the beasts, but before my eyes it was so, when I noticed that the great gates at the southern end of the courtyard were opening. As they opened I saw that beyond them were drawn up a line of men. An officer gave an order, and two machine guns were placed in position in the gate entrance; round the guns lay their crews, and the seething mass of revellers saw nothing. I felt that a fearful tragedy was impending, and as I held my breath with anxiety the officer gave a short, sharp movement with his hand and a hideous rattle rose above all noises. The pandemonium that ensued was indescribable. Some ran helplessly into the burning house, others ran round and round in circles, others tried to get into the dairy; one man got upon its roof and fell back dead as soon as his head appeared above the outer wall. The place was surrounded. It was horrible. A few tried to rush for the gate, they melted away like snow before the sun, as their bodies met the pitiless stream of bullets. I suppose two hundred men were killed in as many seconds. The machine guns ceased fire. Ambulance parties came into the yard, collected the dead and living, and within half an hour there was not a soul save myself in the place. Discipline had received its oblation of men's lives.

As an example, it was one of the most wonderful things I have ever known in your wonderful army, my Karl, but it was terrible—terribly cruel.

I never knew what became of my mother, though I feel she is dead—murdered, perhaps, like my father and my darling Alex, or perhaps she hid somewhere in the house and remained petrified with terror till the flames came. Next morning I left my hiding-place and walked about. Not a German was to be seen, but in the wood was a huge newly-made grave. It was all open warfare then, and this flying column, which was miles in advance of the main body, had moved on. The house was a smoking mass of ruins, but the farm buildings had been spared, and I let out all the poor animals and turned them into the woods, so that they might have their chance.

All day I searched for my father and brother, but not a sign was to be seen, and at dusk I stood alone, faint and broken, amongst the ruins of my ancestors' home. As I looked at this scene of desolation and I contrasted what had been my life twenty-four hours before and what it was then, something seemed to snap in my brain, and for the first time I cried. Oh! the blessed relief of those tears, my Karl, for I was a poor weak, helpless girl, and alone with death and bitterness all round me. Late that night I hid once more in my hay-loft and next morning I left Inkovano for ever. Before I left, I made a vow. It is because of this vow, my beloved, that I am to die. For I vowed by the body of our Saviour and the murdered bodies of my family that, whilst life was in me and the war was maintained, for so long would I work unceasingly for the Allies against Germany. As the war ran its fiery course, I have seen more and more that the Allies are the only ones who will do anything for Poland, my beloved country, so have I been strengthened in my vow.

I struck south on my feet, as a poor girl—I, the daughter of a princely family of Poland! No hardships were too great for me, provided I could reach Allied territory. I travelled from village to village as a singing girl, and once I was driven away with stones by villagers set upon me by a fanatical priest. I came by Cracow, and across the Carpathians, helped to pass the lines by a Hungarian Lieutenant—but I tricked him of his reward; I was not ready for that sacrifice. Then across the Hungarian plains to Buda-Pesth, where I remained three weeks, singing in a third-rate café, to make some money for my next stage. But I had to leave too soon—the old story!—this time it was the proprietor's son. What beasts men are, my Karl! And yet to me you are above all other men, a prince amongst your fellows, and never did I love you so distractedly as that first night at the shooting-box, when I read the scorn in your eyes as you rejected me. I have no shame in telling you this. Am I not already in the grave? And then I must be silent and can only await your coming. After many struggles, wearisome to relate, I came to Hermanstadt, and there, whilst pushing my trade as a dancer, came into touch with a Hungarian band of smugglers, working across the mountain passes between Eastern Hungary and Roumania. I did certain work for these men, and in return crossed with them one bitter night in a thunderstorm into Roumania. At Bukharest I got a good engagement, and when I had saved a thousand marks, I bought a passport for five hundred, and came to Serbia, then staggering beneath the great Austrian offensive.

Once again I was in the horrors of a retreat, but I escaped, reaching Valona, and crossed to Brindisi, by the aid of a French officer to whom I told my story and who believed me. His name is Pierre Lemansour, and he lives at Bordeaux.

If fortune places him in your power, be kind to him, my Karl, for your Zoe's sake.

I came to Rome; and thence to Paris. I stayed here three weeks, singing in a cabaret. Whilst here I tried to advance my plans in vain! What could I, a poor girl, do for the Allies? The Embassy laughed at me, all except one young attaché who tried to make love to me.

Then I thought of England—England, and her cold, hard islanders, phlegmatic in movements, slow to hate, slow to move, but once roused—ah! they never let go, these islanders!

One of their poets has said: "The mills of God grind slowly, but they grind exceeding small."

That, my Karl, is like England.

They are your most terrible enemies, and you know it.

Do not be angry with me when you read this.

For me it is Poland, for you Germany.

Where I am going in a few hours there is no Poland, no Germany, no England, no war. And perhaps, perhaps, no love.

You and I, Karl, have loved, too well, perchance, but our love was above even the love of countries.

God made the love of men and women, then men and women created their countries.

I see the future before me, Karl, and I foresee that the struggle will be at the end of all things, between England and Germany. One will be in the dust.

Thus, I crossed to England and was swallowed up in the great city of London. England has always had a corner of her calculating heart for the small nations, and in London there is a Polish organization. I applied there, and one day I was taken to the Foreign Office, and found myself alone with a great Englishman. His name was—No, I promised, and it will not matter to you, for though he gave me my chance, I have no love for him, and he will never be in your power. Even as I write these words, he has probably taken a list from a locked safe and neatly ruled a red line through the name Zoe Sbeiliez. I tell you they know everything, these Englishmen. I told him my story, and then he asked me whether I was prepared to do all things for the Allies. I told him I was. He then said that I could go as agent for a back area in Belgium, and my centre would be Bruges. I agreed, and asked him innocently enough how I was to live in Bruges. He looked up from his desk and said:

"You will be given facilities to cross the Belgium-Holland frontier, as a German singer."

"And then?" I asked.

"You will go to Bruges and make friends with an Army officer; he must be high up on the staff."

I guessed what he meant, but hoped against hope, and I said: "How?"

I can still see his fish-like face, hair brushed back with scrupulous care, as without a shadow of emotion he looked up, puffed his pipe, and said in matter-of-fact tones:

"You have a pretty face and an excellent figure. Need I say more?"

I could have struck him in the face. I was speechless, my mind a whirl of conflicting emotions. I was roused by the level tones again.

"Is it too much—for Poland?"

Oh! the cunning of the man; he knew my weakness. Mechanically, I agreed. Certain details were settled, and he pressed a bell. Within five minutes I was walking back to my lodgings.

Thanks to a marvellous organization, which your police will never discover, my Karl, within *three weeks* I was singing on the Bruges music-hall stage, and accepted without question as being what I was not, a German artist from Dantzig. The men were soon round me, but I had no use for youngsters with money. I wanted a man with information. At last I found my man—the Colonel. He was on the Headquarters staff of the XIth Army, the army of occupation in Belgium, when I first met him. Subsequently he went back to regimental work; but by the time he was killed (and to realize what a release that meant for me, you would have had to have lived with him) I had established regular sources of information concerning which I will say no more. Let your country's agents find them if they can. This must I say for the Colonel: he was a brute and a drunkard, but in his own gross way he loved me, and he licked my boots at my desire, but I had to pay the price. You are a man, and with all your loving sympathy you can but dimly realize what this costs a woman. To me it was a dual sacrifice of honour and life, but it was for Poland, and the memories of my parents and Alex steeled me and strengthened my resolution, and so, and so, my Karl, I paid the price.

My special work was on the military side, and consisted in making quarterly reports on the general dispositions of large bodies of troops, the massing of corps for spring offensives, and big pushes and hammer blows.

Then you came into my life! When the Colonel used to go away it was my habit to mix in the demi-mondaine society of Bruges, to try and live a few hours in which I could forget—oh! don't think the worst! *That* sort of thing had no attraction for me. I didn't seek oblivion in that direction! I had never even kissed anyone in Bruges until I kissed you that first night we met at dinner—I was attracted to you from the very first; the Colonel was due back in a few days, and I suddenly felt mad, and kissed you. I suppose you put me down as one of the usual kind, out to sell myself at a price varying between a good dinner and the rent of a flat! You will now know that I had already mortgaged my body to Poland.

Then a few days later you will remember we went down for that wonderful day in the forest, and for the first time, Karl, I began to see that I was really caring for you, and a faint realization of the dangers and impossibilities towards which we were drifting crossed my mind.

Do you remember how silent I was on the drive back? In a fashion, my Karl, I could foresee dimly a little of what was going to happen. I had a presentiment that the end would be disaster, but I thrust the idea away from me. Then came the day, just before one of your trips—oh! the agony, my darling, of those days, each an age in length, when you were at sea—when you told me at the flat that you loved me.

How I longed to throw my arms round your neck and abandon myself to your embraces, but I was still strong enough in those days to hold back for both our sakes.

Each time we were together I loved you more and more, and each time when you had gone I seemed to see with clearer vision the fatal and inevitable ending.

But I refused to give up the first real happiness that had been mine in my short and stormy life, and so I clung desperately to my idle dream.

I prayed, I prayed for hours, Karl, that the war might end, for I felt that in this lay our only hope—but what are one woman's prayers, a sinful woman's prayers, to the Creator of all things, and the war ground on in its endless agony just as it does to-night—Karl! Karl! will this torture ever end?

But I must hurry, there is still much to tell you, and Time goes on relentlessly just like the war; it is only life that ends. Then came the days I took you to the shooting-box for the first time, and that night I broke down and, unashamed, offered you myself. Think not too badly of your Zoe, my Karl; when a woman loves as I do, what is convention? A nothing, a straw on the waters of life. I wanted you for my own, passionately and desperately, for I feared that any moment the end might come, and to die without having felt your arms around me would have added a thousand tortures to death. Though I could have welcomed death with joy when I saw the look of sorrowful contempt which you cast upon me that night. Heavens above! but you were strong, my Karl. I am not ugly, and yet you resisted, and I hated and loved you at the same time—oh! I know that sounds impossible, but it isn't for a woman. I slept little that night and, feeling that I could not look you in the face in the morning, I left for Bruges before you got up.

I felt that I could trust you not to try and find out the secret of the shooting-box.

What a relief it is to be able to tell you everything frankly, and how I hated the perpetual game of deception which I had to play.

I used to rack my brains for answers to your perpetual question, "Why won't you marry me?" It was a desperate risk taking you down to the forest, but you loved me so much that you never questioned the reasons I gave you for my secrecy. I can tell you now, Karl, that in the early days when I used to disappear from Bruges, it was to the shooting-box that I went.

But I will write more of that later.

Did you suffer the same agony as I did before you left for Kiel, and your pride would not allow you to come to me? You understand now, my darling, why I could never marry you, and when the Colonel was killed it became harder than ever. Once during that terrible interview before you went up the Russian coast, I nearly gave way and promised to marry you. But how could I? I had sworn my vow, and even to-night, though I stand in the shadow of death, I do not regret my vow.

It is inconceivable that I could have married you and carried on my work—a spy on my husband's country—and if I ever thought of trying to do this impossible thing, a vision which has partially come true always restrained me.

I saw a submarine officer disgraced and perhaps sentenced to death, because his wife had been convicted as a spy!

No! it was impossible.

But if I could not marry you, I still wanted your love.

Then you went up the Russian coast, and I heard of your return in a submarine terribly wrecked. I guessed what you must have gone through, and determined to see you, but when I entered your room and saw you lying open-eyed on your bed, with no one but a clumsy soldier to nurse you, I could have wept. You know the rest; you can perhaps hardly remember how I led you to my car and took you down to the forest. Oh, Karl, are you angry with me for what happened? Do you sometimes think that I took an unfair advantage of your weakness? Please! Please forgive me, you were so helpless, and I loved you so.

Then came those unforgettable weeks whilst your boat was being repaired, weeks which opened to me the door of the paradise I was never to enter. Oh! Karl, I pray that all those memories may remain sweet and unclouded all your life. Think of those days when you think of your Zoe. Alas! they came to an end too soon, and you left for the Atlantic. When you came back all was over; I had been caught at last.

The evidence at the trial was clear enough. I have no complaints. I was fairly caught. You remember the big open space in front of the shooting-box? I do not mind saying now that five times have I been taken up from there in an English aeroplane, and landed there again after two days. Each time I took over a full report on military affairs. Not a word of naval news, my Karl; you will remember I never tried to find out

U-boat information. I even warned you to be cautious. Well, they caught me as I landed; the English boy who had flown me back tried hard to save me, but it only cost him his own life.

My first thought was of you, and there is not a jot of evidence against you, save only your friendship for me. Remember this fact, if they persecute you. Admit nothing, believe nothing they tell you, deny everything; they have no evidence; but they are certain to try and trap you.

It was noble of you, Karl, to engage Monsieur Labordin in my defence, but it was useless and may do you harm.

I also know of your efforts with the Governor. I hoped nothing from him, but what you did has made me ready to die; I tremble lest you are compromised.

If only I could feel absolutely certain that I have not dragged you down in my ruin I should face the rifles with a smile.

For my sake be careful, Karl.

When it is all over, cause a few little flowers to cover my resting-place, if this is permitted for a spy. Order them, do not place them yourself; you *must not* be compromised.

I have told my story, and the end is very near. What else is there to say?

Mere words are empty husks when I try to express my thoughts of you.

Do not sorrow for your Zoe, to whom you have given such happiness.

I am not afraid to die and cross into the unknown, which, however terrible it is, cannot be much worse than this awful war.

Karl! Karl! how I long to kiss you and feel your strong arms crushing the breath from this body of mine which has caused so much sorrow.

Oh, Mother Mary, support me in this hour of trial.

I cannot leave you!

May the Saints guard you and keep you through all the perils of war, and grant that we meet again in the perfect peace of eternity.

For ever, Your devoted and adoring ZOE.

Karl's Diary resumed.

She is dead!

They have killed her, my Zoe, my adorable darling, and I am still alive—under close arrest. Perhaps they will shoot me too, in their insatiable thirst for blood. Oh! if they would! Perhaps, my Zoe, if I could only die and leave this useless world behind, I might find you in the mysterious regions where your spirit now dwells.

Oh! is it well with you, Zoe? Give me a sign—a little sign—that all is well. I have knelt in prayer and asked for a sign, but nothing comes—all is a blank, forbidding and mysterious. Is God angry with us, my Zoe, that we sinned before Him? Surely, surely He understands. He must have mercy on me if He is going to make me go on living. If this is my punishment, I can bear it; I will live without you happily if only I may know that all is well with you.

* * * * *

Your letter, Zoe! Can you read these words as I write; can you sense my thoughts? Speak! Ah! I thought I heard your voice, and it was only the laughter of a woman in the street. Your letter has filled me with joy and sorrow. I read and re-read the wonderful words in which you say you loved me from the beginning, but when you plead that I shall not turn in loathing from your memory—with these words you smash me to the ground.

Most glorious woman, I never loved you so well and so passionately as the day you stood at the trial, ringed round with the wolves, the clever lawyers, the stolid witnesses, the ponderous books, the cynical air of religious solemnity with which the machinery of the law thinly cloaks its lust for blood—for a life.

Even when my ears heard the sentence, I could not believe it would be carried out. The firing party, the chair, the bandage. Oh, God! spare me these awful thoughts. To think of your breasts lacerated by the—Oh! this is unendurable! Stop, madman that I am!

* * * * *

I am calmer now; I have read your letter again and rescued the journal from the grate into which I flung it.

The fire was out; I am not sorry; my journal is all I have left, and in its pages are enshrined small, feeble word-pictures of paradise on earth. To read them is to catch an echo of the music we both loved so well. Music! you were all music to me, my Zoe. Your voice, your movements, your caresses all seemed to me to speak of music.

I ask myself, I shall always ask myself until the last hour, whether all that could be done to save you was done. I tried to telegraph to the Kaiser for you, Zoe, but the wire never got further than Bruges post office; they stopped it, and put me under arrest. It was only open arrest, my darling, and on that last awful night I forced them to let me see the Governor. I, Karl Von Schenk, knelt at his feet and begged for your life. He simply said, "You are mad." I left the Palace under close arrest.

Was ever woman's nobleness of character so exemplified as in your life? Be comforted, Zoe, that in all my black sorrow I cling desperately to my pride in your strength. I long to shout abroad what you did and why you would never marry me, to tell all the gaping world that when you died a martyr to duty was killed. I am so unworthy of what you did for me, my darling, and it tortures me with mental rendings to think that whilst I prided myself in my strength of mind, I was dragging you through the fires of hell. When I think of those six weeks we had together, my brain says, "And they might have been months had you not spurned her in the forest."

Oh, Zoe! if the priests say truth and all things are now revealed to you, forgive me for this act of mine. Come to me in spirit and give me mental peace.

" . . . when there was a blinding flash and the air seemed filled with moaning fragments."

"When I put up my periscope at 9 a.m. the horizon seemed to be ringed with patrols."

As I write like this, as if it was a letter that you might read, I am comforted a little; I rely utterly on the hope, which I struggle to change into belief, that you can read this and know my thoughts.

For when I think that had things been otherwise you might have been leaning over my chair at this moment, and running your cool fingers through my stiff hair; when I think of this, my darling, the full realization comes to me of the gulf which must divide us for some uncertain period, and the lines of this page run mistily before my eyes.

Zoe, my Zoe, strange things have happened in this war; wives declare they have seen their husbands, mothers have felt the presence of their sons; if the powers permit, come to me once again, I implore you, and give me strength to live my life alone.

* * * * *

Examined before the Court of Inquiry to-day. Fools! can't they realize that I don't care if they do shoot me?

In the Mess, people avoid me. What do I care? Not one of them is worthy to stand on the same soil that holds her beloved body. They have buried her in the Castle grounds. In accordance with her wishes, I have arranged for flowers. Perhaps one day when all this is over I may be able to live here and tend the place where she sleeps, free at last from all her cares.

* * * * *

At the Court of Inquiry they tried to cross-examine me on our life together. Dolts! what do they aim at proving? That I loved you? I hardly listened. When they finished the evidence, the President asked me if I had anything to say! Anything to say! I felt like telling them they were cogs in the most monstrous machine for manufacturing sorrow and destruction that mankind had ever devised. I could have shaken my fist in their solemn faces and shouted "Beasts! you murdered her! You destroyed that most wonderful woman who lowered herself to love me."

Actually there was a long silence, and then the Vice-President, Captain Fruhlingsohn, said, "Speak; we wish you well."

It was the first touch of sympathy, the only sign of humanity I had received in all these awful days, and it touched my stubborn heart and the longed-for tears flowed at last.

I murmured: "Gentlemen, I am no traitor; but I loved her as my own soul."

"Dissolve the Court. Remove the prisoner." Like the clash of iron gates, officialdom came into its own again.

* * * * *

So I am not to be shot! Not even imprisoned! "Don't fall in love with enemy agents again!"—that summarized their verdict.

Ha! Ha! Ha! It is all horribly funny. The real reason is that they need me. I am a trained and skilful slaughterer on the seas; I am an essential part of the great machine. And they haven't got any spares! I was in the Mess yesterday when the English papers we get from Amsterdam arrived. Oh! a pretty surprise awaited the first man who opened *The Times*. These English had published the names of 150 U-boat commanders they had caught. There they all were. Christian names and all complete. The only thing missing was a blank space in which to fill in our names when the time comes.

Dinner was a silent meal last night, and next morning some rat of a Belgian had posted the list on the gatepost of the Mess. The machine has offered five hundred marks for his apprehension—how foolish; as if by shooting him they would take any names off the long list.

* * * * *

I am to sail at dawn tomorrow. I shall not be sorry to get away for a space from this place with its mingled memories of delight and death.

* * * * *

Back again, and I haven't written a word for three weeks.

My billet last trip was off Finisterre. I sighted two convoys, but there were destroyers there; they are so black and swift I don't go near them.

I don't want to die in a U-boat. It's not worth while. It is easy to avoid these convoys. I dive and make a great fuss of attacking, then I steer divergently. Nobody knows where the enemy is except me; I am the only one who looks through the periscope—I take good care of that. And then how I curse and swear when I announce that the convoy has altered course, and there is no chance of getting in to attack. None of them are so disappointed as I am!

The mines get on my nerves, there is no way of dodging them, and Lord! how they sprout on the Flanders coast.

I am to go out in six days. It is very little rest. I believe they want to kill me. But I won't die! Not I.

I went to her grave yesterday for the first time. I had thought I should weep, but I did not; in fact it left me quite unmoved. I feel she's not really dead; she comes to me sometimes, always at night when I am alone and when we are at sea. There's nothing very tangible, but I catch an echo of her voice in the surge of the sea along the casing, or the sound of the breeze as it plays along the aerial. And so I will not die until she calls me, for up to the present her messages have told me to live and endure.

* * * * *

A very awkward incident took place last night. We were off the Naze and saw a steamer some distance away.

We dived to attack. When we were about a mile away I had a look at her, and something about her put me off. I half thought she was a decoy ship, and I privately determined I would not attack. I steered a course which brought me well on her quarter, and as soon as I saw that it was impossible to get into position to fire I increased speed on the engines and shook the whole boat in efforts which were ostensibly directed to getting her into position. At length I eased speed and bitterly exclaimed that my luck was out.

The First Lieutenant suggested that we should give her gunfire, but I pointed out that I had good reason to suspect her of being a wolf in sheep's clothing, and as he had not seen her he could hardly question my judgment. I was going forward, when I accidentally overheard the Navigator and the Engineer talking in the wardroom. I listened.

The Engineer said: "The Captain doesn't seem to have the luck he used to command."

"Or else he has lost skill!" replied Ebert. "We never fired a torpedo at all last trip, and it looks as if we are following that precedent this time."

I had heard enough, and, without their realizing my presence, I returned to the control room. I considered the situation, and came to the conclusion that they suspected nothing, but it was evident that their minds were running on lines of thought which might be dangerous. I looked at my watch and saw that there was still two hours of daylight left, and then decided to play a trick on them all. I relieved the First Lieutenant at the periscope, and when a decent interval of about half an hour had elapsed I saw a ship. This vessel of my imagination, a veritable Flying Dutchman in fact, I proceeded to attack, and, after about twenty minutes of frequent alterations of speed and course, I electrified the boat by bringing the bow tubes to the ready.

The usual delay was most artistically arranged, and then I fired. With secret amusement I watched the two expensive weapons of war rushing along, but destined to sink ingloriously in the ocean, instead of burying themselves in the vitals of a ship. An oath from myself and an order to take the boat to twenty metres.

With gloomy countenance I curtly remarked: "The port torpedo broke surface and then dived underneath her, the starboard one missed astern."

So far all had gone well, but ten minutes later I nearly made a fatal error. We had been diving for several hours, the atmosphere was bad, and as it was dusk I decided to come up, ventilate, and put a charge on the batteries. I gave the necessary orders, and was on my way up the conning tower to open the outer hatch. The coxswain had just announced that the boat was on the surface, when a terrible thought paralysed me, and I clung helplessly to the ladder trying to think out the situation.

It had just occurred to me that as soon as the officers and crew came on deck they would naturally look for the steamer we had recently fired at; this ship in the time interval which had elapsed would still be in sight.

As I came down, the First Lieutenant was at the periscope, looking round the horizon. Quickly I thrust the youth from the eyepiece, and, as calmly as I could, said: "I thought I heard propellers."

Half an hour later we surfaced for the night. I have been wondering ever since whether they suspect, for the three of them were talking in the wardroom after dinner and stopped suddenly when I came in.

I must be careful in future.

* * * * *

I was sent for this morning by the Commodore's office, and handed my appointment as Senior Lieutenant at the barracks Wilhelmshafen.

No explanation, though I suspected something of the sort was coming, as three days after we got in from my last trip I was examined by the medical board attached to the flotilla.

So I am to leave the U-boat service, and leave it under a cloud! It is a sad come-down from Captain of a U-boat to Lieutenant in barracks, a job reserved for the medically unfit for sea service.

Am I sorry? No, I think I am glad. Life here at Bruges is one long painful episode. No one speaks to me in the Mess. I am left severely alone with my memories. The night before last I found a revolver in my room, and attached to it was a piece of paper bearing the words: "From a friend."

Perhaps at Wilhelmshafen it will be different, and yet, when I went down to the boat at noon and collected my personal affairs and stepped over her side for the last time, I could not check a feeling of great sadness. We had endured much together, my boat and I, and the parting was hard.

At Barracks.

As I suspected when I was appointed here, my job is deadly to a degree, and my main duty is to sign leave passes.

Our great effort in France has failed, and now the Allies react furiously. The great war machine is strained to its utmost capacity; can it endure the load?

Our proper move is to paralyse the Allied offensive by striking with all our naval weight at his cross-channel communications. The U-boat war is too slow, and time is not on our side, whilst a hammer blow down the Channel might do great things. But we have no naval imagination, and who am I, that I should advance an opinion?

A discredited Lieutenant in barracks—that's all.

Worse and worse—there are rumours of troubles in the Fleet taking place under certain conditions.

It is the beginning of the end!

Last night the High Seas Fleet were ordered to weigh at 8 a.m. this morning.

A mutiny broke out in the *König* and quickly spread.

By 9 a.m. half a dozen ships were flying the red flag, and to-day Wilhelmshafen is being administered by the Council of Soldiers and Sailors.

There has been little disorder; the men have been unanimous in declaring that they would not go to sea for a last useless massacre, a last oblation on the bloodstained altars of war.

Can they be blamed? Of what use would such sacrifice be?

Yet to an officer it is all very sad and disheartening.

I have seen enough to sicken me of the whole German system of making war, and yet if the call came I know I would gladly go forth and die when *tout est perdu fors l'honneur.*

Such instincts are bred deep into the men of families such as mine.

We approach the culmination of events. To-day Germany has called for an armistice. It has been inevitable since our Allies began falling away from us like rotten print.

The terms will doubtless be hard.

* * * * *

Heavens above! but the terms are crushing!

All the U-boats to be surrendered, the High Seas Fleet interned; why not say "surrendered" straight out, it will come to that, unless we blow them up in German ports.

The end of Kaiserdom has come; we are virtually a republic; it is all like a dream.

* * * * *

We have signed, and the last shot of the world-war has been fired.

Here everything is confusion; the saner elements are trying to keep order, the roughs are going round the dockyard and ships, looting freely.

"Better we should steal them than the English," and "There is no Government, so all is free," are two of their cries.

There has been a little shooting in the streets, and it is not safe for officers to move about in uniform, though, on the whole, I have experienced little difficulty.

I was summoned to-day before the Local Council, which is run by a man who was a Petty Officer of signals in the *König*. He recognized me and looked away.

I was instructed to take U.122 over to Harwich for surrender to the English.

I made no difficulty; some one has got to do it, and I verily believe I am indifferent to all emotions.

We sail in convoy on the day after tomorrow; that is to say, if the crew condescend to fuel the boat in time. Three looters were executed to-day in the dockyard and this has had a steadying effect on the worst elements.

* * * * *

I went on board 122 to-day, and on showing my authority which was signed by the Council (which has now become the Council of Soldiers, Sailors and Workmen), the crew of the boat held a meeting at which I was not invited to be present.

At its conclusion the coxswain came up to me and informed me that a resolution had been carried by seventeen votes to ten, to the effect that I was to be obeyed as Captain of the boat.

I begged him to convey to the crew my gratification, and expressed the hope that I should give satisfaction.

I am afraid the sarcasm was quite lost on them.

* * * * *

We are within sixty miles of Harwich and I expect to sight the English cruisers any moment.

I wrote some days ago that I was incapable of any emotion.

I was wrong, as I have been so often during the last two years.

In fact, I have come to the conclusion that I am no psychologist—I don't believe we Germans are any good at psychology, and that's the root reason why we've failed.

I do feel emotion—it's terrible; the shame—the humiliation is unbearable.

I wonder how the English will behave? What a day of triumph for them.

The signalman has just come down and reported British cruisers right ahead; it will soon be over. I must go up on deck and exercise my functions as elected Captain of U.122, and representative of Germany in defeat. One last effort is demanded, and then—

NOTE
This is the last sentence in the diary. It is probable that he suddenly had to hurry on deck and in the subsequent confusion forgot to rescue his diary from the locker in which he had thrust it.

ETIENNE.

BIBLIOBAZAAR

The essential book market!

Did you know that you can get any of our titles in large print?

Did you know that we have an ever-growing collection of books in many languages?

Order online:
www.bibliobazaar.com

Find all of your favorite classic books!

Stay up to date with the latest government reports!

At BiblioBazaar, we aim to make knowledge more accessible by making thousands of titles available to you- *quickly and affordably*.

Contact us:
BiblioBazaar
PO Box 21206
Charleston, SC 29413

CPSIA information can be obtained at www.ICGtesting.com
Printed in the USA
LVOW10*2013211213

366353LV00004B/183/P